CULTIVATING

HOPE

CULTIVATING
HOPE

WEEKLY READINGS TO OPEN
YOUR HEART AND MIND

Karen Casey

HAZELDEN

Hazelden
Center City, Minnesota 55012
hazelden.org

Library of Congress Cataloging-in-Publication Data

Casey, Karen
    Cultivating hope : weekly readings to open your heart
  and mind / Karen Casey.
        p.   cm.
    ISBN 978-1-59285-736-4 (softcover)
    1. Hope—Religious aspects. 2. Peace of mind. I. Title.
    BV4638.C375 2009
    242'.2—dc22

                                                        2009022015

Editor's note
The names, details, and circumstances have been changed to
protect the privacy of those mentioned in this publication.

    This publication is not intended as a substitute for the advice
of health care professionals.

    Alcoholics Anonymous and AA are registered trademarks of
Alcoholics Anonymous World Services, Inc.

13 12 11 10 09   1 2 3 4 5 6

Cover design by David Spohn
Interior design by David Swanson
Typesetting by BookMobile Design and Publishing Services

Dedication

I want to dedicate this book to all the men and women who have inspired me to be hopeful, sometimes in the face of very difficult circumstances. Without the hope I have been blessed with, I would not be able to pass it on to others. That's the beauty of hope. To keep it, we must be willing to give it away to those who are looking to us. In this way, the circle is made whole.

"Hope arouses, as nothing else can arouse,
a passion for the possible."
WILLIAM SLOANE COFFIN JR.

Contents

$\sim\!\!\sim$

$\sim\!\!\sim$

⌒⌒

⌒⌒

$\mathcal{C}\!\!\sim\!\!\mathcal{O}$

$\mathcal{C}\!\!\sim\!\!\mathcal{O}$

Acknowledgments

My mind moves in so many directions when I think about all the people who have been important to me on my journey—people who have inspired hope in me when I was lacking in hope—and every one of them is a part of this book in some way. But first, I must acknowledge my Higher Power, whom I choose to call God. I didn't easily gravitate to believing in God in the early days of my sobriety, but I have "dodged too many buses" not to fully believe, now, that He was always present.

Next on my list is my husband, Joe. He has never failed to encourage me when I needed it or to help me see the lighter side of life when I have gotten too serious. My many women friends—Connie, Kaye, Joy, Joan, Alida, Sylvia, Barbara, Jane, Mary, Julie, Anne, Terri, Margaret, Peggy, Mike, Tessa, Lisa, Kathy, Sandy, and Kit, just to name a few—have been absolutely instrumental in carrying hope to me, laughter to me, and a solid sense of the presence of God in their lives, too. When we see God in other "skins," we know we can rest easily.

I want to acknowledge my friends who shared their own stories of hope with me so that I could pass those stories on to you. And I want to acknowledge my many friends at Hazelden as well. My work as a writer began at Hazelden nearly thirty years ago, and I am so grateful for the continuing opportunity to be in their "stable of writers." I am particularly grateful to Sid Farrar for seeking me out for this book. I have respected his work at Hazelden for many years, and working with him again on this book was a pleasure.

Last, but certainly not least, I want to acknowledge my family for their continuing love and support. And even though my parents have passed on, I feel the flutter of their wings on many occasions and I know they hover, passing on the peace of their love to me as I continue to navigate through this world.

Introduction

Why write a book on hope? I've given this question careful consideration, and the more I ruminated about the topic, the more compelled I was to write about it. Perhaps that's because my life is now a testament to hope. When I wandered into the rooms of Al-Anon and Alcoholics Anonymous nearly thirty-five years ago, I was bereft of hope—and I didn't even know it. I was simply numb and confused, and I wanted someone to save me, preferably another relationship partner.

I had always tied my dreams and what hope I had to having a significant other, one who would adore me, comfort me, and never reject me. But I had failed to capture that person, except for short spells. Surprisingly, my first marriage lasted twelve years, probably because my husband was as insecure as I was. Every relationship that followed was much shorter-lived. I simply didn't understand that relationships were partnerships. I wanted to hold someone hostage, forever. As one rejection followed on the heels of another, I became more desperate, and the solace I sought from alcohol and drugs took center stage in my life.

When I walked into my first Twelve Step meeting in 1974, I had no idea what was in store for me or what my future held. I went at the suggestion of a counselor. I stayed because I sensed that the men and women in the room felt as I had always hoped

1

to feel. They laughed easily and hugged often. They listened to one another intently. They seemed to truly care. And they talked about hope and its availability to any one of us who really wanted to make different choices. I can remember wondering what they really meant when they talked in those terms. All I really wanted out of life was for *others* to change, which I felt would ensure my security. Hearing that it was *me* who had to change was not easy to accept or understand. But I stuck around anyway.

Since that time so many years ago, I have discovered, and bathed in, the awesome power of hope. Along with the ever-necessary willingness, hope is the trigger that can change every perspective one holds dear. And the hope that each of us passes on just may be the trigger that can help heal all members of the human community in time—not just ourselves, not just those close to us, but people we will never meet or know were touched by our lives.

What is it about the vision of hope that gives it all of this power? I'm not a believer in absolutes, but I think hope opens our minds to possibilities that have always existed but that we have not entertained because of fear. When hope opens the door to these possibilities, we have to decide if we want to change or live as we have always lived. Giving up the known for the unknown is not a decision made lightly. Fortunately, we have the example of others to help us see the prudence in following our hearts and making the change that will lead us to a better experience now and tomorrow.

I am grateful to be surrounded by people in recovery who have been led by this vision of hope and who have made this choice to change, again and again. While not everyone reading this book will be in a Twelve Step program where change is a necessary constant, everyone has been touched at some point in their lives by people who have followed their hearts and made changes that grew out of a feeling of hope for something different. I think it's incumbent on those of us who have been led by our experiences with hope to serve as examples to others that change is possible for them, too.

In fact, I'd go one step further and say I believe that everyone sharing in the message of this book has somehow been selected to show others that there is another way to think and live. Perhaps it sounds a bit grandiose, but I think we, as believers in hope, can take the reins and usher in real change, change that just might be felt across the earth if we allow ourselves to cherish hope, rather than hopelessness, about our lives and the world as we perceive it.

One of the most important concepts I have been introduced to over the last three decades—and it's a concept that's consistent with many spiritual paths—is that all members of the human community are interconnected. Even modern science supports this reality. We are not separate entities. We are not even separate from the "stuff" of our environment. Our egos push us to think we are separate, and in the process, they push us to compete, to argue, to create wars big and small. But we are One. With all that exists, we are One. And by embracing hope, we have an opportunity to align our thinking with this idea. When we have done so, when we see ourselves as joined with our fellow travelers everywhere, we discover a peace that indeed *surpasses all understanding.* Most of us have to first develop hope that this is even a possibility, however. And it is *my* hope that this book can be helpful in doing just that.

I write about love and how its expression heals the one who offers it as well as the one who receives it. I write about anger and how understanding the true nature of anger is key to changing our outlook. Realizing that holding judgments against anyone also holds us hostage is illustrated throughout the book. Comprehending that everything we experience can be the pathway to a more hopeful and peaceful life allows us to celebrate rather than dread whatever comes our way. The stories introducing each month's reflections show how the lives of twelve people have been dramatically changed through the power of hope. These individuals faced many obstacles in life, but they refused to give up on hope and drew on the hope that others nurtured for them, lending credence to my belief that hope is possible for us all.

This book is an invitation to embrace a radical but, I believe, necessary idea: *our experiences are all necessary and have been invited by us at an earlier time and place.* We are always where we need to be, sharing space and time with others who are part of our destiny. People who are able to understand and then apply these principles can ultimately realize an inner peace that's so complete that others are changed by their very presence.

This process of seeing anew isn't something that happens overnight, and it may require painstaking effort at times. We didn't get where we are now all at once. We won't get to where we want to be without patience, commitment, and a little willingness. If you take one principle and its accompanying essay and focus on it for a week, letting it inform your habits and your

4

thoughts for that time, you may find that you have begun to move from your old way of seeing, *and being,* to a way that is far more helpful to yourself and others. We don't change our old ideas easily—nor should we. We need to make informed choices about our behavioral and attitudinal changes. Too often, in our past, we let the ideas of others decide for us willy-nilly what we would believe. I am not offering these ideas for you to adopt unless they fit for you. But I do invite you to find out whether or not you feel better about your potential, about your journey, about your fellow travelers after practicing the suggestions and reading the stories of success contained in this book.

The time is ripe for change. The world seems to be in turmoil, and I think it's because many of us are in turmoil, too, that our inner world is manifested in the outer world we share. But I also think cultivating hope will lead to inner peace that can anchor us in a mind-set that says, "I can see a better day ahead, for me and for those I love." If every one of us reading these essays and stories of hope actually believed this and gave it a try, we could positively affect any number of the people who travel our path with us every day. Our interconnectedness makes this indisputable. And everyone we affect with our new vision of hope will be encouraged to see differently, too. If we want a different life, a different set of experiences, a different, more hopeful world, we must be agents of change. There is no better time than now. Won't you join me in this effort?

How to Use This Book

How you use this book is ultimately up to you, but here are a few suggestions: The book is divided into twelve themes,

one for each month. Each month begins with a story of hope
followed by an essay, or reflection, for each week. Additional
reflections are included on page 181 for those months that
have an extra week in a given year. I have chosen these stories
because of how moved I was by them. Gathering stories from
others has always been one of the joys of my recovery. It's my
hope that they speak to you as they spoke to me. Knowing
that others have overcome unfathomable odds allows us the
privilege of holding on to the belief that we can do the same
and then pass on our stories of success in turn.

The essays for each week can be read once at the beginning of the week or daily, if that's helpful. It's always been my
experience that reading an essay one time seldom implants it
firmly in my mind, so I do recommend repeated readings. I
have also made a few suggestions to consider for the month,
which are in keeping with the theme. You might make notes
for yourself or journal about your progress at the end of each
day or week. If you have another approach that works better for
you, please use it. Let us do whatever allows us to move forward
with hope and enter each day, each week, lovingly and with
help on the tip of our tongues. We can truly make a difference
in the lives of everyone we encounter, whether we've known
them for years or have only just met them for the first time.

You'll note, too, that the essays' themes are repeated a
number of times. That's quite intentional. Spiritual perspectives, particularly if unfamiliar to us, bear repeating many
times to be fully heard, fully absorbed, fully applied. And
this book is intended to change us so that we might serve as
examples to others who might also desire to make changes

in their lives. A friend suggested to me many years ago to approach new spiritual beliefs like mantras, repeating them gently to myself until they feel comfortable, like soft slippers. I found my friend's advice to be extremely valuable, not only because it allowed me the time I needed to incorporate new direction but also because it was kind and loving and forgiving of my many missteps on this new path I was traveling. If the repetition of a particular theme or idea troubles you in any way, simply move on to the next essay or repeat an earlier one. This book should never frustrate you. It's written to offer you solace, direction, and hope. Nothing more but certainly nothing less.

Additionally, there are very few really new ideas, regardless of how many books make a claim to the contrary. I don't want you to think I am suggesting that these ideas and themes are original. They aren't. My knowledge and wisdom have come from many sources, my Higher Power being the primary one, and it's my firm belief that what has come to any one of us is to be given away if we want to keep it for ourselves. We are all part of a healing circle. No one of us is separate from it. Your work, like mine, is to pass on to others that which you have been moved by, changed by, healed by. It's clear that we are here, in this time and place, intentionally. I am delighted to be part of your journey.

Please know that my prayers are with you as you travel this path. It takes all of us to make this a world that each of us can truly thrive in. May you find peace.

January

HOPE

Make yourself necessary to someone.
RALPH WALDO EMERSON

How Much More Can One Person Take?
With Hope in Your Heart, a Lot!

Terry wasn't the first person in her family to have a problem with alcohol, but she was the first one to be officially diagnosed as alcoholic. However, this didn't occur until after she had left a state facility for the mentally ill. Her family had had her committed because they didn't know how to deal with her incessant acting out, and they wanted to get her off the streets. It never occurred to them to have her assessed for alcoholism or drug addiction; doing so wasn't common at the time. The facility didn't recognize her addiction, either. They saw her as mentally ill, period. The facility wasn't a refuge, though, as she was abused and raped during her stay, an incident that enraged her for years. No one believed what had happened, even her family, but at that time and in that place, many things were often overlooked.

Many of Terry's problems with her family stemmed from

her accusation that her father was an alcoholic. Hers was a large Catholic family with lots of drinking and many alcoholics, but naming the problem was against unspoken family rules. Her dad reacted, of course, and so did all the other drinkers in the family. No one wanted to be singled out, so everyone came to his defense, lest they be named next. No one was. Terry was soon institutionalized, and life went on.

When Terry was eventually released, she returned to her former ways, and her drinking and drug use escalated. Some of her siblings joined her now on her escapades. This lifestyle couldn't last long, however, because she couldn't hold down a job. She bunked with friends here and there, but she soon wore out the welcome mat. She abused not only drugs but also her friends, and they turned away from her; she was just too much to handle.

Having no place to go, she wandered into a home that housed runaway kids. There she met the person who became instrumental in her salvation from a dead-end life. He was a gentle man who understood addiction and who listened to her. He didn't think she was crazy, but he did think her problems were more complicated than just addiction. She trusted him, and together they began exploring what help she really needed. The first thing her new friend did was contact her parents, letting them know she was safe. Initially, she resisted, but he promised he wouldn't let them commit her again and that he would help them understand what her struggles were. And here is where recovery eventually began, not just for Terry, but for others in the family, too.

Terry's mother was relieved. Her dad was skeptical; he

had his own addiction to protect, after all. But into treatment Terry went. That, coupled with the proper diagnosis of a treatable mental condition, gave Terry a new start on life. The outpatient treatment program she attended had the reputation of being hard core, and that was just what she needed. The program not only helped her become sober but also gave her the foundation that has supported her sobriety for more than thirty-five years. Unfortunately, she hasn't been free of other conditions, ones that might have pulled a less hopeful person off course.

Her first serious condition was the diagnosis of manic depression, or bipolar disorder. Though it's commonly diagnosed and treated today, back then many didn't understand the disease or its treatment. And the recovery community didn't support the use of any kind of drug, for any reason, even one as legitimate as what Terry needed to function in the world. Fortunately, she had a counselor who helped her understand how crucial her medication was. Terry continues to take this medication and lives a life free of mania and depression.

She was advised to go off her medication during her two pregnancies, and she experienced psychotic episodes both times. These experiences were harrowing, but she came through them with the help of understanding doctors, a family who finally accepted her condition, and a husband who was trained to administer to these circumstances. Since that time, she has been episode free and comfortably sober.

Were her story to end here, it would still exemplify the power of hope. But there was and is so much more to Terry's story. About ten years ago, she was diagnosed with cancer of the pelvic bone. She had experienced pain in her hip for more than a year but had assumed that it was a strained muscle from exercising too much. Doctors and physical therapists treated her symptoms but didn't look for an underlying problem. When the cancer was finally diagnosed, major surgery was immediately ordered to remove part of her pelvic bone. The operation took a team of doctors most of a day, and she was put in a body cast that she would need to wear for the next twelve months. Twelve months totally incapacitated!

With two young children and a marriage straining under enormous pressures, she lived one day at a time, moment by painful moment. The chaos that had hounded her mind before she was diagnosed with bipolar disorder returned, not because of the disorder this time, but from the circumstances of a life totally beyond her control.

Terry owes her survival of this ordeal first to the tools of her recovery program and next to the people who came to help with her daily needs. They cared for her children, assisted with her personal needs, and relieved her of the feeling that survival was all on her shoulders—shoulders literally locked into a body cast. Even though her husband was still in her life, he was having difficulty coping with the many changes to his marriage and family. Few of us are taught strategies for dealing with the kinds of enormous complexities that Terry and her family faced. Her family of origin helped as much as possible, but they, too, were ill equipped to deal with these conditions.

In a book on hope, I'd like to say Terry had plenty of it throughout her convalescence, but that wasn't always the case. There were many hopeless days and even weeks. That she maintained her sanity throughout the constant chaos and sadness over this turn of events means that someone was holding out hope for her while she struggled to muster any herself. That's one of the key messages here: one person having hope keeps the flame ignited and inspires others to nurture hope in their own hearts. Many people were drawn into the circle of hope for Terry. Recovery meetings were carried to her home as readily as were meals for her children. She was never abandoned to her fears about her condition and her future.

Doctors couldn't guarantee that when the cast came off she'd be able to walk, at least not without crutches. Her worst fears were realized, in fact. She has not been able to walk unaided and never will be able to. Since getting the cast removed, Terry has moved many times, trying to find a home that accommodates her needs. Quietly and resiliently, her family has moved as well, and Terry continues to handle a seemingly impossible position with grace, even with wit.

But the story doesn't end here. Two years ago, with the return of intense pain, doctors performed surgery again. They believed Terry might be a candidate for a new prosthesis. For a while, it looked like they were right, and she proudly walked, a tiny bit, using just one cane. But the experiment didn't prove to be effective for very long. Terry is now back to the wheelchair and occasionally the crutches.

Stress fractures are taking their toll on her body but not her mind. Miraculously, she looks at her life with gratitude every day. And this gratitude strengthens her. Terry's story demonstrates that any situation is survivable if we are willing to allow for the gift of hope being offered by others. Tragedies may live in the chaos of our minds, but we don't have to be ruled by them. We can, instead, take charge and live fully in spite of our challenges. Terry now has a car equipped with a lift, and she is out and about, at meetings, at lunch with friends, at the grocery store. It is a privilege to watch Terry and to be able to pass on what she teaches us. She is a living example of what we can do if we gather the hope of others and couple it with a belief in a Power greater than ourselves.

January Suggestions for Cultivating Hope

1. Find or buy a small notebook or journal that you can keep with you, in a pocket or purse or backpack. During this month, list examples of ways other people demonstrated hope in their lives that you were privileged to observe. Write as much or as little as you like; a line or two describing each example is usually sufficient.

2. Make a note of the times you offered the hand of hope to someone else. Describe how giving to others in this way lifted your own spirits.

3. If someone reaches out to you when you are feeling afraid or troubled in any way, make a note of it at the end of the day (or even right after the help was offered). Help is constantly available if we avail ourselves of it.

4. At the end of each week, review what you have written and ask your Higher Power to help you become even more observant.

One Can Be Hopeful or Judgmental, but
Not in the Same Moment.

Negative judgment is a topic I'll turn to numerous times in this book because of how much harm it inflicts in our lives. It hurts the one sitting in judgment, the one being judged, even those merely perceiving its occurrence. And yet we all judge; no one is immune. In our families of origin, many of us felt the sting of judgment on a regular basis when we were small, often unfairly—so the die was cast. We learned to recognize and then to mimic this behavior. As a consequence, hope was often in short supply.

Wherever two or more are gathered, the opportunity for passing judgment may rear its ugly head. Holding back our judgment—letting those in our homes, at work, even strangers live free of our judgment—takes both vigilance and willingness. My own experience is a testament to this.

Lest I be misunderstood, not all judgment is bad; there are no absolutes. For example, a judgment has been rendered when we decide to help another person. We make the "judgment" to see another person's needs as worthy of our concern. And offering suggestions to others based on our personal experiences, and then letting go of what they do with the suggestions, is judgment of another kind. Judgment in these instances is not harmful.

So how does hope relate to judgment? As already stated, we can't hold judgment and hope in our minds simultaneously. One has to be relinquished. Unfortunately, it is often hope that we give up, perhaps because of its unfamiliarity. However, one moment at a time, we can make the commitment to release the negative and nurture hope instead. It begins with a decision, perhaps to do something as simple as asking a friend to be hopeful *for* us. (Two minds are always better than one.) The idea of making the decision to be hopeful may seem ludicrous, but we have to begin somewhere.

It has been helpful for me to reflect on the past and note where my journey took a turn for the better in spite of me. I believe that Someone was in charge, and it wasn't me—perhaps acting through someone else who was holding out hope for me. I am convinced that there is and always has been a *Presence* who was keeping me safe. And I have hope that this Presence will never leave my side.

Hope is elusive, only because it isn't treasured enough. It can become as strong in our lives as any other characteristic. Start by seeing hope as a muscle that needs to be exercised. Then practice strengthening it in small ways. For instance, muster some hope that you can finish a small task that you have been putting off and ask a friend to offer you some of her hope as well. Hope can help us to accomplish any feat. Beginning small and experiencing success will be the impetus we need to see how it will help us achieve our dreams.

Hope isn't mysterious. We simply haven't taken
advantage of it. Today we can.

Being Hopeful Opens the Door to Real Possibility.

Feeling hopeless about a situation in your life makes all forward movement seem impossible. It's not an accident that we have people around us who can share our sorrows and express hope for us when our own is depleted. Our lives are quite intentional. You've probably heard it said that nothing happens by accident. When we're down, another person appears who can show us the rainbow that's hidden from our view. She didn't appear by chance. She had an assignment. You fulfill that "assignment" on occasion, too, for others.

I like believing in angels, both ones wearing skin and ones "from the other side." The nudging we get from them when it's time to give up a worn-out idea just can't be ignored. We might not let the idea go willingly, but our "messenger" persists until we acknowledge the nudge. Instead of fighting it, we can see it as the inspiration to welcome new opportunities into our lives. We aren't passing through this experience haphazardly. We have guides, and we have assignments. We have others who need our presence to show them the way, too.

Knowing that we are never alone in our struggles is reason for hope. Nothing will ever be beyond our capabilities because so much help surrounds us. Much of it we can't see, and we often ignore the signs that are always there. But the people who wander into our gatherings, large or small, have always been invited. What an awesome awareness. We don't always appreciate the "wanderers." That's okay. They don't need our appreciation to do their work.

It reminds me of an "angel" who came to my rescue nearly thirty-five years ago. Her name was Pat. I had flirted with the idea of suicide hundreds of times since childhood, but I was never closer to taking action than I was this time. I had even laid out what I needed on the kitchen table. And then a stranger knocked at the door, interrupting my plans. It was an insistent knock. Reluctantly, I opened the door, and as Pat entered, my life changed. The details of this experience aren't what's important for now (and I'll share them later); what is crucial is that I didn't know her. Even though we had apparently made an appointment to talk, proof that she shared with me from her calendar, I had no knowledge of having met her before.

After a short time together, Pat left, and my world had shifted. She was the symbol of hope that had died in my life. What she shared with me about the hopeless state I was in had a ring of truth to it. I knew from the story she shared that God was waiting for me to finish the work I had been called to do. Pat was my bridge to the other side of the dark abyss. I have thought about her many times over the years, but I never saw her again. All that I have done since that fateful day is owing to her rescue. She saved my life by igniting hope in me where a void had been. Ever since, I have considered it part of my work to try to pass on hope to others.

Passing on hope may be little more than offering the hand of friendship to a stranger. Sometimes, it's merely taking the time to pray with a friend, or alone on her behalf. Holding hope in our hearts for those who are lacking it is the easiest way we can make a difference.

Hope Is the Pathway to Getting What You Want Out of Life.

I didn't know what I wanted out of life. Primarily, I just wanted someone to notice me, to love me, to promise to never leave me. I wanted someone to make me the center of his life just as I had made him the center of mine. I look back on those years with embarrassment, and yet I simply didn't know who else to be. My role models struggled with the same issues.

And then I was introduced to recovery and the idea that I could make other choices for how to be and how to view my relationships. I was astounded to realize there were myriad ways to perceive situations that attracted my involvement, ways that didn't put me *or the other person* at the center of the experience. I was also astounded to realize I didn't need to live my life around anyone else's choices anymore—only my own.

I saw many people at many Twelve Step meetings who described how hope had encouraged them to make better choices, improving every aspect of their lives. I knew that if they could do it, so could I. I kept listening and changing. And hope, first theirs and then finally my own, became my inspiration.

I never expected to do what I have ended up doing with my life. But that tiny word, *hope,* opened my mind and then the doors to the journey I continue to make and cherish. This isn't something that only happens for a few of us, let me assure you. Hope is a gift to all of us. If we struggle to find hope during difficult times, others are available to help us. We now know that hope can be taught. Emphasizing our strengths, letting them take the lead in our decisions for self-care, will create in us the potential—the hope—we need to make the changes that can help us get what we really want out of life.

When used as a therapeutic method, this is called Hope Therapy. But it doesn't need a clinical label to be valid and important—it's something we all can learn to do in our everyday lives. We all have strengths. Even when our ability to see them is clouded by our defects, they still exist. It may be necessary to ask others to help us see them at times. If so, see that as intentional, because it's a gift to ask others for that kind of help. We travel together because we are supposed to be helping each other. It's a give-and-take that benefits us all.

I have discovered that one of my strengths is "hearing" the message behind the message that someone is sharing. I believe God has made this a possibility for the work I have been called to do. You have been called to do your own special work. If you don't think you are presently doing it, seek to know your strengths. If you can't recognize your strengths right now, ask your fellow travelers what they see.

*Getting what you want out of life and getting
what God wants you to have might run on opposite
tracks for a time. But when you have hope and a
willingness to be your better self, the two "wants" will
come together. Your life's real work depends on it.*

When People Are Unkind, It's Usually
Because They're Afraid.

This might well be one of the most accessible principles we can use when faced with people who are difficult—work colleagues or phone solicitors or shoppers pushing their way through the grocery store, for instance. Some days, difficult people seem to be everywhere. And yet, there are some people who insist that no one is really difficult. This was true for my aunt, who died last year at age ninety-nine; it was her philosophy that people who appeared hard to deal with were simply having a bad day. She considered encounters with them an opportunity to say something extra nice. She said doing this made her feel good. I am confident her comments eased their struggles, too.

I've never met anyone who was more peaceful than Aunt Helen. She had a radiance about her that caught your attention, and people, young and old, loved being with her. She lived a joyful life even though she had lost her husband early in life and had to raise six children alone. She told me she never felt the need to remarry because she was filled to the brim with love for her husband, Leo. She never felt sorry for herself and never looked at others in anger or with envy.

Her way of seeing the world makes sense, I think. She lived her life in a way that, both directly and indirectly, passed on hope to others whether they were in crisis or just in need of comforting words. How often do we fail to notice the many people around us who are struggling? How frequently do we turn away when a smile might make all the difference to someone feeling sad or afraid? Probably often. If we consider that people who aren't connecting with us might be afraid, this makes for potentially very different and kinder encounters. Reconsidering what kind of response we might make to someone crossing our path could be the turning point in both of our lives.

I was exposed to what anger can do to a person in my family of origin. All the time I was growing up, I had no idea that fear was likely at the root of it. Had I understood how insidious fear could be and how it could infect every dynamic of a family, I would have been far more forgiving of my father's rage. Fortunately, before his death, I learned from a woman far wiser than me about the depth and the meaning of the struggle that had controlled his life. My compassion for my father fostered my willingness to have greater compassion for others, too. From every circumstance, we can glean important information that will make the rest of our journey smoother.

Anger can be interpreted as a catalyst for kindness, which in turn paves the way for a more hopeful journey. This idea might seem like a stretch at first, but it has changed my life in significant ways. Hope can seem to be in short supply in our world. Making a space for it anywhere is worth the effort.

Our encounters with others need never be dreaded
or judged. They simply are, and accepting them
and the lessons they bear make us the hopeful guides
the world is waiting for. Hope can be created from
nothing more than willingness. Being kind is one
element of the change the world needs.

JUDGMENTS SEPARATE US

He who angers you, conquers you.
ELIZABETH KENNY

〰️

Working an Eight-Hour Shift Was More Than a Rude Awakening.

Jeff had been a drug dealer most of his young adult life and had never held a real job. He wasn't just a dealer, however—he used as much as he sold and had been doing so since he was fifteen. In fact, what he sold merely kept him flush enough to buy what he needed to stay high. He was going nowhere fast. And then the bottom fell out: His parents told him they were no longer willing to support him, house him, or bail him out of jail. At about the same time, his girlfriend dumped him. With few options, Jeff agreed to go to treatment. He really didn't plan to stay clean and sober; he just wanted the heat off him and figured he could tolerate anything for a while.

The severity of Jeff's addiction demanded more than a month of inpatient treatment. So after completing that segment, he transferred to a long-term facility where recovering addicts could stay for up to six months. This is when our paths crossed three months later, when it was assumed Jeff was ready to take on some responsibility. I worked for an organization that gave job experiences to recovering addicts, and Jeff was assigned to work in my department.

Jeff's first day on the job was memorable, to say the least. I offered some direction to this man whose eyes were at half-mast, explaining what he needed to do and to whom he would report. Although I could tell he didn't really understand my words or the task I asked him to do, he nodded and walked away. I asked his supervisor to keep an eye on him. It wasn't hard—he moved very slowly.

It was customary to break in the "employed" patients gradually, since many hadn't held a real job for some time, if ever. The first two weeks they worked only half days; Jeff managed to be present most of these hours. By week three, a six-hour day was expected. Jeff seemed to find six hours on the job trying; concentrating on tasks this long was pretty hard for him. But he gave it his all, and he wasn't altogether un-successful. Week four brought full, eight-hour days, and this pushed him over the edge. He wasn't as ready as we'd hoped. Midafternoon of the first full day, his supervisor discovered him asleep at a desk in the far corner of the warehouse. When she woke him, he seemed surprised and incredulous that tak-ing a nap on the job wasn't permitted.

No doubt, had this been a "normal" work situation, Jeff would have been fired, but the organization I worked for and the treatment facility he lived in had agreed to a trade-off: free labor in exchange for teaching job skills. Jeff wasn't dumb. He simply didn't comprehend the importance of being responsible and didn't understand that others were counting on him to complete his tasks. We didn't give up on Jeff, although the temptation was there at times. As he continued on the job, he grew in his willingness to be more responsible.

When his six months in the treatment facility were up, Jeff said he wanted to stay on the job. I, for one, was surprised. There were far easier ways to earn a living, but Jeff seemed to truly want a new beginning. He applied for the job, knowing that, as a paid employee, the rules would no longer be so lax. No more naps in the warehouse; no more showing up late for work. We took a chance and officially hired Jeff, and none of us ever looked back. Over time, Jeff became a valued employee, working in many capacities over the years. Long after I left the organization, he remained as more than just a great employee and became an ambassador for the organization.

I stayed in touch with Jeff because he had really touched my heart. The contrast between the man who showed up that first day of work, with eyes at half-mast and slow speech, and the person he became when he fully embraced recovery was astounding. His was a success story of epic proportions. He was transformed from a drug dealer and addict—someone whose life was going nowhere—to a man with a clear mission, one that matched that of the organization he worked for.

Jeff and I had forged a connection when he was selected to work in my department. There are no accidents. Whom we meet is by divine selection, and even more than that, we can be certain that we are being sent the people who will stretch us to new heights. I never expected to learn anything from Jeff; how wrong I was. I learned how laying my judgments aside gave both of us the freedom to become who we really needed to be. This is a principle that can be applied by anyone, anywhere.

Through this experience, I also learned that gently having hope and expectations for others can help them rise to the occasion. Hope is a wonderful elixir. It promotes willingness and inspiration. When we hold out hope to others who are struggling to experience it on their own, we are offering them a lifeline. I still remember and cherish what some of my women friends did for me many years ago at one of my first large speaking engagements. I was a bit unsure of myself, so my friends came en masse to support me. Before I walked to the podium, one of them said, "Remember, we will hold hope along with your heart in our palms as you speak." As I began my talk, I looked at my friends in the back of the room, standing there with outstretched hands. I was comforted and hopeful and able to move through my talk with ease. Allowing others to have hope for us benefits them as well as ourselves.

Offering hope to people who have none may seem foolish, perhaps, but it can and will make a difference in the outcome of their struggle. I have seen it work many times. Jeff is a great example. So many of us held out hope for him until he could develop it on his own. Because of his gentleness, his likability, and his commitment to what our organization stood for, he had many cheerleaders. He was the embodiment of our mission, and he saw his role on its behalf as the most important work he could imagine doing.

It was a sad day when Jeff left the organization and returned to his hometown to care for his ailing parents, a mom and a dad who had literally saved him from himself. He watched over them until their deaths with the same love and commitment he had demonstrated in the organization he had grown to love. Never did his parents have to doubt that he'd be there. He knew he had a debt to pay them and was only too glad to pay it. He felt privileged, he told me, to do for them what they had done for him.

Unfortunately, not many years after his parents died, Jeff was diagnosed with the same disease that had claimed their lives. He was circumspect about it, however. He had a way by now of putting things into perspective. That's one of the countless blessings of long-term recovery. Jeff didn't feel sorry for himself and was certain that he'd had "a good run." He also felt confident that he'd meet up with his parents on the other side, and there he'd wait until his wife and the rest of his friends joined him.

The last time I spoke with Jeff was only days before he died. I was so glad for the opportunity to tell him what knowing him had done for me. He had shown me that no one is hopeless, that everyone has a unique journey, and that my part of the equation, with those I meet, is to lay my judgments aside and let God show those people to me as they really are. Jeff left life just as he had left the organization, feeling both love and hope that the next part of his journey would match, in every way, what the best of the preceding parts had been. He told me he was ready to move on, and I could hear the resolve, and even anticipation, in his voice.

Those of us who knew Jeff well will not soon forget him. All that he lacked when he walked toward me the first time

27

we met, he developed in spades by the time he died. Hope was at the core of his life, not only hope for himself but for every person he met who struggled as he had. That's the value of sharing our lives, isn't it? We learn from those who journey with us today so that we can teach those who will journey with us tomorrow. Jeff was a great traveler, a great student, and an even better teacher.

February Suggestions for Cultivating Hope

1. Being judgmental is a habit and one that can be changed. See how many times over this next month that you can interrupt judgmental thoughts and replace them with thoughts of kindness, if not toward the person you are with, then on behalf of someone else. Make a note of each attempt in your notebook.

2. Practicing gratitude for the many people who cross your path, knowing they are there by divine appointment, is an easy way to change how you feel about your inter-actions. At the end of each day, take a moment to journal about how your heart changed when you allowed grati-tude to fill it.

3. Being judgmental toward anyone changes how we treat everyone. Look for all of the times you seek to see the good qualities in others. At the end of each day, write down at least one experience where you looked for the good.

4. Our judgments hold us in bondage. Releasing even a tiny one allows us a sense of freedom. Getting a taste of this

freedom makes it easier to do it again. What judgment did you let go of today and with whom?

We Are Held Prisoner by Our Judgments and by the Judgments of Others.

How many thoughts do you have on a daily basis that are clearly negative judgments of yourself or others? If you're like me, you probably have hundreds of them, many of them so subtle they almost go unnoticed. Admitting this about ourselves isn't easy, but it's true. And while we might not see ourselves as fearful, fear must play a role in our lives, or we wouldn't be playing judge and jury on others' lives.

Classifying all actions as examples of either love or fear, simplistic though that may seem, forces us to acknowledge that our judgments certainly aren't loving expressions. Loving actions are always easy to identify. They are usually quiet, easy, and kind, and they are most frequently offered to people who are also kind—although the most truly "productive" loving actions might be offered to the more difficult people in our lives.

The action I most resist taking full responsibility for, and that frankly embarrasses me, is when I silently observe others, wishing they were different. Because I am saying nothing in these instances, it's easy to pretend that my behavior isn't hurting anyone. How wrong that assumption is. Any judgmental thought we entertain is holding us hostage. If a thought is negative, it's harming us, and it's creating a force field of negativity *29* around us, a force field that radiates out to everyone else.

We affect others by our thoughts and by our moods, as much as by our actions. Because we seldom see the ramifications of our inner thoughts and unexpressed moods, we can and often do deny their harm. And yet, how often do you leave a gathering feeling ill at ease or worse because of the mood of the group? Words don't even have to be spoken for the impact to be felt. And they seldom are, in fact.

What can one do to change all of this? Honesty and recognition of what our minds are really harboring is the first step. The second step is to transform any thought that is less than loving to one that is. If you can't think of a loving thought in that moment, think of a compassionate, loving God. Filling our minds with the goodness of God—whatever image that conjures—fills our hearts with hope, which is followed by gratitude that we aren't really at the mercy of a mind that's out of control. Not unless that's our choice—and it's a safe bet it won't be.

We do have the personal power to make any change we want to make, in thoughts, actions, or feelings. Our minds reflect our wishes. Do we want peace? Do we want to be expressions of love? Do we want to cherish hope as the way to the life we deserve? Nothing stands in the way but ourselves. Harboring judgments is little more than a bad habit. Nothing can keep us from developing a better habit from this moment forward.

Opening the prison door is not that difficult.
The key is in one's mind. Now is a good time
to use that key and enjoy the freedom
that awaits on the other side of the door.

30

No One Is on Our Path Accidentally.

How often do you really look, with focused intention, at the people you see in the halls at work or in line at the grocery or on the street as you wander by? Most of us do see other people, but quite unconsciously. We need not be ashamed of how easily we dismiss the presence of others; it's usually not deliberate. We are simply self-absorbed. The good news is that we can cultivate the belief that each person is offering us an opportunity to connect on a spiritual level. Joining with each person in this way, by making intentional eye contact, has an immediate healing effect on us and on them, too.

When we seek to see the *Spirit* in others in this way, strangers as well as friends, we are taking the first and very necessary step to becoming aware of *that Spirit.* In many cultures, looking into other people's eyes is the highest honor we can pay them. Becoming committed to doing this increases our peace of mind while showing others that they matter to us, too. Honoring others in this way may not feel natural at first, but if they have crossed our path, this is what we have been called to do.

Not all of our meetings are pleasant, yet they are all vastly important. Take a few moments right now to think of a handful of difficult people you have encountered in your life, perhaps recently. Are you able to glean the lesson that was being offered in any experience that comes to mind? It may not have felt very nurturing. Many of them don't. But these are lessons that make up the points on our journey that are nudging us forward. And if we aren't moving forward, we are stuck in the past, where we've cut ourselves off from God.

Each of those people we have met has been kept alive by the same spiritual flame that keeps us alive. Remembering this can help us recall these difficult experiences and these people with a different level of acceptance. We are on an equal footing. Try thinking of anyone who wanders into our lives as someone seeking to be both teacher and student within the encounter we are about to share. Perhaps we will still ignore someone's presence from time to time, but if there's an important lesson to be shared between us, we will encounter one another again.

You may have had experiences you resist thinking of as necessary lessons. I have some in my past, too. I have come to the conclusion that I don't have to understand why an experience had value for me to believe that it did. What I do know is that I now travel a peaceful path most days, and I have not had to deny any experience that occurred. I know that the painful ones were teaching me something important that I needed to pass along to someone else. We never know how we are being used by the God of our understanding. We only know that *we are being used.* That brings great relief.

> *We certainly don't know what the day may bring,*
> *but we can be certain that God is part of what*
> *unfolds. Any experience will be used many times,*
> *and not just by us. That's the hopeful reality.*
> *Whatever comes to us will be shared many times*
> *to the benefit of others. Our being fully present*
> *is the key to the unfolding of the mystery.*

*The Real Hope for Humankind Relies on Our Seeing
That All People Are Essentially the Same.*

This world of six billion includes people with so many personalities and of so many different cultures that it may seem a real stretch to say we're all very much alike. Surely there are few similarities between an Australian Aborigine and an Iowa farmer. And can we really believe that England's royal family is truly like a poverty-stricken family who lives in a one-room shanty in the hills of Kentucky? In order to accept this particular principle, we have to *think and see* beyond each other's outward appearance. We are so much more than our physical bodies. Relying on the "body" to tell the whole story of humanity is like equating the bricks and mortar of a church with the Spirit of God that resides within each worshipper.

We have been "schooled" to believe that external appearance tells us everything there is to know about someone. Back in the sixties, men with long hair and sandals were potential anarchists, according to certain people with different political views. And watching the Amish in their buggies on the back roads of Indiana and Ohio, a man wearing a two-thousand-dollar suit and driving a Mercedes is unlikely to be heard to say, "We are really alike!"

There truly is so much more than meets the eye. It is what's inside each person that matters: this is how and where we are the same. That's where Spirit lives, and we all possess the same Spirit: both the destitute woman begging on a Manhattan street corner and the wealthy Fortune 500 CEO looking down from the corner office above her; both the angry runaway

33

teenager and the desperate, confused parents waiting at home. When we can finally begin to see how alike we are at our core, we will be able to appreciate the value in both sharing our burdens and celebrating our successes with all comers. We no longer need to compare ourselves as better than or worse than someone else, and we may find ourselves saying, "We are alike. We all have fears, we all hurt sometimes, and we share the planet to both give and receive help. Let me help you, in this moment, because I know I will be helped, too."

If it still feels too much of a stretch to accept that we are the same as those who appear radically different, begin by trying to lay all judgments aside for just one day, or even one hour. Looking deeply into the faces of those who travel on this path with us can be our starting point. Making the attempt to see the presence of Spirit in someone else will be enlightening. It will certainly help us, as the viewer, to see beyond the clothes or the physical appearance of the person who stands before us. It will give us the sense of being seen as well.

Beginning to see how we're the same as others
moves us closer to change. We must begin somewhere.
The health of our planet, and all of us who share it,
demands no less. Giving up our inclination to always
judge the other person is another principle that will help
us feel more hopeful about every aspect of our lives.
And we will have offered the greatest gift we can,
that of hope, to someone else.

Our Interconnectedness Means That What We Do to One Person, We Do to All.

This principle might be hard to grasp, even unimaginable, but many great thinkers, spiritual voices from all disciplines, and philosophers both living and dead are in agreement that we humans are not separate physical entities, isolated and unaffected by the actions of others; rather, we are very much connected, within ourselves—mind and body—and to other living beings. In concert, we—*all of us*—make up "the fully connected whole" of humankind. This gives us reason to rejoice. It means we are not alone as seekers, alone as journeyers, alone as problem solvers. Instead, we are sharing a vision for our lives with six billion other people. And when the vision of this collective mind includes peace, there is great hope that it will come to pass.

We can experience great contentment in knowing that our journeys are not isolated—singular and wholly independent—but take on their purpose and meaning when experienced intentionally in concert with those we walk among. We can rest assured that, because of our connection, we will not be "left behind." The corollary to this is that anytime we attack another person, through words or deeds, we are hurting ourselves along with the person we intended to harm and creating the illusion of separation. But when we remember that there is no separation between us, we can assume that a loving word or deed can bring happiness not only to the giver and the recipient but also to the countless others on their paths.

Our lives in every detail—all that we think with our minds, all the words we say, the actions we take, even the unspoken images that cloud our minds—affect other people eventually. It's not just the people in our families and our colleagues at work who are affected, but also everyone affected by these people, eventually rippling across the world and impacting people whom we will never meet. They will all be touched by what we do and say and think, right here, right now. In physics, it's called the butterfly effect, and the same spiritual principle also holds sway over us whether we acknowledge it or not. Celebrating this effect by adding goodness to the world through our words and thoughts is offering a mighty gift to all of humankind every day.

There is great potential for goodness in our lives, and thus in the world, when we put into practice the power for good that's available to each of us. Remember, we are collectively doing for everyone what we do for anyone. That means every time we have a hope-filled thought or prayer for someone else, we have included ourselves and all of humankind as the recipients, too. Just consider for a brief moment the power of our tiny actions. The repercussions are phenomenal. As Margaret Mead, the anthropologist, said decades ago, and I paraphrase: If you think one person can't change the world, think again. That's how change happens: one person, one hopeful thought at a time collectively changing the world.

Going through each day with this knowledge at our
fingertips gives us both the courage and the inspiration to
make a difference in the lives of everyone else, a difference
that will affect us as well. Having one good thought is
all that's necessary. How simple is that? One thought
of hope for humankind promises a positive outcome for
all of us. Let's grab this idea and run with it.

March

GOD'S WILL

*In the transformation and growth of all things,
every bud and feature has its proper form.*
FRITJOF CAPRA

Has the Merry-Go-Round Made Its Last Stop?

Janet was one of sixteen kids born to alcoholic parents
who didn't fend well for themselves or their children. All sixteen were removed from their home on the Indian reservation
in early childhood. Because there were so many children, they
were split up and placed in various foster homes throughout
the state.

Janet and two of her younger sisters were placed in the
same foster home. Yet this home proved to be dangerous as
well—all three girls were abused both sexually and physically.
After similar experiences in two or three homes, and with no
one to turn to for help, Janet ran away for the first time when
she was thirteen. She learned how to shoot craps in dark al-
leys to earn money for food. Pretty soon, she learned there
were other ways to earn it, too. And the alcohol she was given
helped her forget how she got paid, at least for a time.

Janet knew she'd be in trouble for running away, but she didn't care. Living on the streets was preferable to being a victim, again and again, in homes she hated and where she felt hated, too. At least on the streets, she had more control over her victimizers. What worried her the most was how her younger sisters were faring. Janet couldn't forgive herself for abandoning them.

None of the children fared well. The ravages of alcoholism claimed eight of Janet's siblings. Some committed suicide; two died on the streets; others simply died. Janet's parents both died in their early fifties—neither had ever been able to stay sober. Her dad finally shot himself, and her mother died from complications of alcoholism.

Meanwhile, Janet experienced a few relatively successful years in adulthood, albeit not entirely sober ones. Still, she did work in a professional setting for several years. She was smart, and she impressed people with her wit, her intelligence, and her relatively consistent dependability. She hasn't changed much through the years—she is still smart and hasn't lost her wit—but her hard years of drinking, drugging, and homelessness have taken their toll.

I met Janet about twenty-five years ago at a recovery meeting. At that point, she had been in treatment multiple times, had spent many weekends in detox units, and had served ninety days in a workhouse. She has been a staple in my life since our first meeting; however, there have been brief periods when I didn't know where she was, or even if she was still alive.

Janet's journey in recovery has indeed been rocky. Her first treatment, nearly thirty-five years ago, was unsuccessful if measured by continuous abstinence. The next eighteen treatments offered her something, I'm sure; however, until her last treatment—in a state-run facility that she was committed to, followed by time in a long-term halfway house—she had managed only a few months of sober living at any one time.

That Janet has experienced a troubled life is clear, but I want you to know Janet more completely so you can understand why I view her story as a truly hopeful one. What she shows us, I think, is that we should never underestimate the power of the human spirit when it is coupled with the Power of one's Creator. What Janet has in this respect, we all share.

For years, I have marveled at Janet's willingness to come back to our fellowship, again and again. There was never a doubt that she wanted what many of us had, because she kept returning to us; she simply couldn't resist the urge to drink when it hounded her. A month here and there of sobriety was all she could manage before the urge to use consumed her mind. The consequences of Janet's relapses in her adult life were substantial. She neglected her children when they were small; her career suffered; and her marriage ended. Ironically, she had been married to a man whom she'd led into a life free from alcohol. He has now celebrated nearly thirty years of sobriety because Janet encouraged him to seek what she simply couldn't maintain for herself.

But the worst of Janet's life has yet to be shared. Four years ago, she suffered a life-threatening brain injury while living on the streets in New Mexico, where she had recently gone through another treatment program only to relapse a few months later. With no job or money and few friends, she began living in a park with other people who were homeless. From there, it was a swift trip to jail, where she was clubbed in a drunk tank and left to die. Fortunately, someone finally came to her aid, emergency surgery was performed, and she was put on a bus and sent north to a daughter who didn't really care if her mother lived or died.

At this point, Janet didn't really care, either, and it wasn't long before she was back doing what she had always done. The disease is awesomely powerful, and it had its grip securely on Janet. For two more years, she was drunk more often than sober. She underwent two more brain surgeries, and her kids turned away even more. Fortunately, some of her friends stood with her, or she wouldn't have made it. Of this she's certain, and so am I. The final straw for her family came when she brought crack into her daughter's home and smoked it in front of her five-year-old granddaughter. Her family committed her. Janet was enraged but helpless. The state took over, and her current journey as a sober woman finally began, or so most of us thought.

But after nearly two years of clean and sober living, Janet started gambling, and the cycle of addiction began yet again. After three months of drinking and hiding, having seizures and begging, she once again has turned her life and will over to a Power that loves her far more than she has ever loved herself.

Janet is currently safe and sober, living in the home of loved ones. Several times a week, she still suffers seizures from her brain injury, and she struggles to speak sometimes. But she is back at meetings, and whenever she shares her experience, strength, and hope with others, she stands as a miraculous example of what can happen when we finally surrender to the Power that is always waiting for us to notice its presence. For this moment, she is gratitude personified.

Fortunately, Janet hasn't lost her wit. When she does find her voice, she easily draws men and women around her because she speaks with such clarity about what she's been through and what life is like now for her. Her story is unlike most. She has come back from the dead multiple times. Janet is a living example that God's Power is not to be doubted. There is a plan for our lives, and that plan will be fulfilled. However, God does wait for our willingness to pay attention. I am grateful that Janet became willing once again. I am not sure how long her willingness will last, but for the moment, she exemplifies the miracle of what even a tiny bit of willingness can do.

March Suggestions for Cultivating Hope

1. The evidence of how God's will has been present in our lives is easy to see if we look for it. Thinking back to your childhood, write down a few examples from your own life.

2. God's will doesn't always make us happy in the moment. Make a note of one situation that has shown you the value of retrospection. What appears to be bad can often be regarded as a positive experience later.

3. No one ever crosses our path by accident. Can you recall an interaction in your past that was full of intention, even though you didn't recognize it at the time?

4. It is God's will that we do our part to make this a more peaceful world. At the end of each day this month, write down one thing you did to promote peace.

We Never Need to Feel Hopeless.
Our Higher Power Is Always Present.

Feelings of hopelessness can creep into our lives through innumerable personal situations. You have been diagnosed with a terminal illness with only months to live, or a parent dies unexpectedly. Maybe your troubled teenager is on the run again, and you feel you have nowhere to turn. The job you have loved for years suddenly gets cut without warning. Or the boss who understood your personal struggles and insecurities and willingly worked with you gets transferred. Or the situation that so many of us dread: your partner or spouse informs you that he or she wants out of the relationship you had believed would be lifelong.

It's easy in any of these cases to fall into despair. If someone responds by saying, "This too shall pass," we may want to scream. *But we never need to feel hopeless. Our Higher Power is always present.* We want the situation that caused our pain to change, however. Now. We want the diagnosis to be incorrect, the parent to live indefinitely, our child to be safe and asleep in her bedroom. We not only want the job to be secure, but we want that big promotion. And we want the "love of our life" to stay committed to this relationship for the long haul, through thick and thin. That's what seems fair, after all.

But life has a different way of showing up, doesn't it? In reality, life shows up as it should. Our lessons are many and intentional—they have not come to us by accident. We have been part of the selection process, whether we know that or not. That's why *we never need to feel hopeless. Our Higher Power is and always has been present.* Cherishing that as our reality can change the way we view every situation in life. The difficult ones are designed to stretch us, to help us reach out to others and to God for support, understanding, and wisdom. The joyful ones are meant to be shared so that our traveling companions will see that life does give all of us moments free from turmoil.

The more we trust that our Higher Power will always do for us what we can't do for ourselves and the more we realize that the many experiences calling to us are our "dancing lessons" paid for by God, the less anxiety we will feel. We will also know that we have been prepared for whatever appears next on our agenda. Rest assured, we have been prepared. Nothing happens that hasn't been divinely ordered. Our lives are never hopeless. We are in the right place, at the right time, walking with the people who are necessary to our journey. And our Higher Power is and always has been present, even when we were certain we had been forgotten.

> *Throughout this week, use the following for a morning and evening meditation:* I need never feel hopeless. My Higher Power is and always has been present. *The cracks in the pavement will become smooth when we rely on this Power for all our answers.*

Wherever We Are Is the Next Right Place to Be.

What great comfort there is in knowing that we are not necessarily "off course," even when it feels as though we are floundering. What seem at first to be missteps can actually be new and unexpected opportunities that are *wearing our name* and have been waiting for us. Perhaps you have experienced a time such as this in your life—I certainly have. When I lost my way in the maelstrom of alcohol, drugs, and the devastating ending of my first marriage, I couldn't fathom that a far more rewarding door was being nudged open for me. Now I understand that I had to be where I was in order to appreciate where I am now.

This is not new information, I'm sure, but recognizing that this has been true for us, *always,* takes an act of will, perhaps. It's natural to forget this principle when we're faced with unsettling turmoil or even during quiet moments in our lives. We know that nothing stays the same, ever. Relationships change, jobs come and go, people die or move on. Health challenges inevitably take us by surprise; depression and fear can crowd out peace of mind in a fleeting second. It's not easy to welcome the idea that we are always in the next right place when nothing feels settled and serene in the moment.

Taking this idea on faith is what we finally have to do. Learning how to fully trust this idea in every instance requires willingness. I didn't have the willingness at one time in my life. In the early days of my recovery, I didn't have the clarity of perspective to see that a *Power* was present in my life and that this Power had always been there, the same Power that I now comfortably take for granted. Now I know, without a shadow of a doubt, that I am perfectly "in place," doing exactly what is next on the agenda for me. Each one of us has an assignment. I am doing mine, and so are you. So is everyone who crosses our path today.

My friend Janet is also fulfilling her assignment. Although she has struggled for more than three decades to be clean and sober, today she is on the path to a clean and peaceful life. It's my prayer that she stays on this path for the remainder of her life, but I know I have to let her path be hers and her Creator's. It's not my journey, but hers. I can pray for her, I can hold a place of hope for her, and I do. But wherever she is, it is her next right place to be. I have to be satisfied with knowing that I always have a way to contribute to the healing of Janet and others, which adds benefit to my life while it adds to theirs, too. It's one of the pleasures of simply living according to God's wishes, a decision you have no doubt made or are considering, or you would not be reading these words. It's a powerful contribution, isn't it? What we do that benefits others makes our lives better, too. The circle is unbroken.

Benefiting someone else by our thoughts and
prayers for them is God's work for us today.
We are in the right place to do it. It's the very work
that changes the world, here and far away.
What an inviting, awesome assignment.

Offering the Hand of Peace to Someone Else Today
Is What Will Transform the World.

How well I remember my fear about entering a room of "strangers." I was certain that everyone was looking right at me, judging my worthiness, and I was sure I was not measuring up. This fear goes back to my childhood, when I so often stood on the outside of circles, both wanting to be noticed and not wanting to be noticed. Sound familiar? By habit, many of us are quite selfishly focused. Our fear keeps us from reaching out to others. Our fear and self-absorption may be deeply ingrained, and it may be our most frequent reaction. Yet with effort, we can pay attention to those people who are, with intention, entering our space.

Once again, the people we encounter are there because they are necessary to the drama we "ordered." We need these people for the lessons we are going to offer each other. They have been invited by the Spirit within, who knows our needs. And remember, we are not interacting with anyone alone. Our Higher Power is always present and has always been part of *our very perfect drama.* The assignment includes all of us who have shown up at a particular place at a specific time.

I remember hearing a noted Jesuit priest and author, share a wonderful story about himself nearly three decades ago. He said he had always been afraid every time he gave a seminar, even though he had given hundreds of them. It was his life's work, in fact. Then one of his mentors suggested that his fear grew out of his need to be loved. He told the priest his job was to offer love to the people who came to his seminars.

Period. With this thought, he said, his fear left him immediately. I took those words to heart, as I knew they described my struggle, too.

Try to make a practice, on this very day, of reaching out to everyone you see, whether you know them or not. Your Spirit knows everyone already. This is a comforting thought, isn't it? We are never in a room with strangers. Everyone is already known by the Spirit within. I discovered the value of this in my work. By greeting everyone who comes to an event where I am speaking with a handshake and a smile, I immediately feel as though I am in the company of friends. Such connection allows for the exchange of ideas we have been readied for.

We make our lives so much more complicated than they need to be. It's not that life doesn't throw us curveballs; rather, it's that we don't have to let them interfere with our stride. If we remember the strength that comes from having hope that all is well, that everything is happening as has been orchestrated, we will receive every experience with the ease and gratitude that it deserves. It's no more difficult than we choose to make it.

Make today an exciting one for you and everyone you meet. Reach out with the love that you have been guaranteed, and you will be making the difference that can change the world. You are not alone. You are the change agent that's needed to make this a more peaceful experience for everyone.

Every Encounter Is Holy.

In every encounter, we are meeting the specific traveler who has been called to our journey. What a wonderful realization. This may well be the most hopeful awareness we will acquire on this path of recovery. *Whoever comes our way is God-sent, and the meeting is divine.* Knowing this to be *Truth* allows us to rest peacefully, assured that we will be able to handle those people who come into our lives and the myriad situations that come with them. What a tremendous wellspring of hope and joy this can be!

God's will is sometimes obvious, sometimes elusive. But it's always within our ability to handle and, in time, grow from. Being willing to see difficult co-workers or irritable clerks as "God-sent" and as offering us an opportunity for forgiveness—both of them and then our judgments about them—is instrumental to the growth we are here to claim. With God's help, we can and will claim it. Even those experiences that deeply trouble us, such as a failed relationship or a runaway child, come with the promise that God is available to see us through. We are never left in a state of hopelessness, unless by choice.

We can rejoice that, if we choose to experience it, hope abounds in all situations, large and small, frivolous or grave, because God is present in each one of them. We can experience hope for peace with our fellow travelers, for the understanding of their plight and our own, for the willingness to allow others to understand us so they can help us on our journey. We do see, when willing, that hope comes in many packages, and every single one of the packages has been handed to us by God, to be unwrapped, never alone, but with His help.

You can probably recall feeling alone at some time in the past during a frightening experience. Most people can. But you weren't alone. What a relief to know that in the worst of times as well as in the best of times, God was already there—we didn't have to issue a formal invitation. This new knowledge means that fear about an experience, or a person's comment, or an upcoming engagement, or a task we feel unprepared for doesn't have to push us under the covers. We can handle everything because we have been assured of the holiness of each situation, every encounter, and the companion we will share it with. God is the guiding force. Nothing happens that doesn't have the element of holiness about it. The sting is gone when we remember that.

We don't have to remember God for God to remember us. His remembrance of us is a guarantee. How fortunate we are that we have never been forgotten and we will never be forgotten. Over this we can rejoice. This is our "ticket" to living the hopeful life, every day.

Every day is offering us opportunities for hopefulness.
And every opportunity is holy, too, because God
is present in the experience. Nothing will
overwhelm us if we remember this.

April
LETTING GO

I think I must let go. Must fear not, must be quiet
so that my children can hear the Sound of Creation
and dance the dance that is in them.
RUSSELL HOBAN

Beginning Again, and Then Again.

Don reclaimed his life, twice. It might be more accurate
to say he is still reclaiming it. The road for this recovering alcoholic has been rocky, not so much because of his drinking,
but because his other addictions have created many hurdles he
has had to climb over, step around, or wend his way through.
He is not a quitter, however, and he is determined to get his
former life back. After listening to his story more than once,
I have become convinced that he will succeed. I am equally
convinced that there are parts of his former life he may never
be able to fully reclaim.

Don is an alcoholic and a sex addict. Born in the Midwest,
he explored many religious and spiritual disciplines over the
years, from Catholicism to Judaism, at many prestigious uni-
versities, traveling extensively in his pursuit of God, education,

and experience. His commitment to social justice and human rights lived at the core of his very being.

While studying for the ministry, he met and married a woman who was following the ministerial path, too, and life looked very promising. Don was successful in his chosen field and was soon looked up to by many. He was a devoted husband and a loving father of four who prided himself on this type of success as well. But Don had his dark side, a very dark side, and it was that side that ultimately derailed him.

After thirteen years of intermittent binge drinking, both before and during his marriage, Don sought help in Alcoholics Anonymous and turned his alcoholism over to the care of a loving God. He has been sober ever since. However, his addiction to sex has cost him everything he ever held dear. In fact, he might say that his other addiction intensified when he found relief from his compulsion to drink.

Although it didn't happen immediately, it wasn't long before his obsession to view Internet pornography and his need for sexual encounters with prostitutes became his whole focus in life. The liaisons with prostitutes had been going on for years, but the Internet pornography was what set the stage for his final fall from grace within his family and community. Until Don had Internet in his home, his wife had been spared those particular details of his dark side. But a few years ago, the facade of his "normal" life collapsed. No longer was he able to keep his two lives separate. Within a few weeks, the marriage, the job, the home, the reputation, the friends, and his children were gone. To date, he has not regained any of them.

But this is a book about hope, and that's where this story

takes us next. Even though Don has lost all that was dear, he has not lost his desire to be of service to others. He knows that can best be done, for now, through the rooms of the recovery fellowships he belongs to. He shares his experience, strength, and hope with others who have stumbled as he has stumbled. Fortunately, he entered a treatment program for his sexual addiction and has made the commitment to carry the message that recovery from sexual addiction is possible. But the shame he feels for having put his family through so much, the shame he feels for having let his church and his friends down, remains.

Healing comes through reaching out to others. That's one of the first things we learn when we begin the journey of recovery. And Don has had the opportunity to help others in truly significant ways. It's not easy to admit one's dependence on alcohol or any drug, but admitting you're addicted to sex with prostitutes and other related behavior can be humiliating. We have heard it said that an addiction is an addiction is an addiction, but are all addictions created equal? Perhaps not. There does seem to be a double standard when it comes to sex addiction. Maybe that's why, even though sex addiction is an illness that touches the lives of millions of addicts and their loved ones, it's hidden in the shadows and on the fringes of society. It's not an addiction that's easily discussed except with other sex addicts. Unlike most other Twelve Step meetings, even the locations of recovery meetings are not widely available. Despite the stigma, sex addiction is an illness that deserves our compassion, our understanding, and our willingness to forgive whatever one's transgressions have been.

Hearing Don tell his story in a very public setting, in a gut-wrenchingly honest and open way, before people of all walks of life—some in recovery who might have had an inkling about his path and some who just happened to be present—was impressive and a bit daunting. He didn't shy away from revealing exactly who he had been. He was also very clear about the work he had done already and where he was intent on going. And that's the key, I think. People who have survived the downward path of destruction must know what they want for their future in order to head in a new direction.

I noted the faces of those who listened to Don's story, and I could tell that some were uncomfortable with his honesty. Sexual addiction isn't as "allowable" as drug or alcohol addiction in this society. But in the final analysis, the differences between various addictions are minimal—it's the drug of choice that's different. Changing some aspect of our reality by altering our brain chemistry and creating the illusion of pleasure and control is the driving force behind any addiction.

That Don is pursuing his profession in the ministry again shows a perseverance that's both admirable and hopeful. He knows that God does for us what we can't do for ourselves, but he also knows that we have to do some of the footwork ourselves. Don is willing to do all that's necessary to regain whatever he can of his former life. He may never win back the love of his family, but having hope for forgiveness spurs him on. He also knows that sharing his story with those who may still live in the shadows of sex addiction has the potential to make a real difference in their lives. It may lead one person to seek help when he would otherwise continue to hide who he really is. Secrets are what keep us sick; they must be shared if we are to heal. Sharing them with even one person opens the door toward the path of healing.

Even though Don is still anguished about what his behavior did to his wife, his children, his parishioners, and his friends; he knows he can't undo the past. He can experience a different present and future, though, and that's what he has set out to do, one day at a time. Don has an easy way about him now. He makes his presence felt in so many ways, offering the hand of healing wherever he can. That's the sign of hope we all crave, no matter what our circumstances. No one is better able to show us that we can come back than someone like Don, who had so much and lost it all. What he has learned and is now ready to share is that like taking a drink, visiting a porn site is only a temporary fix. At long last, he is honestly interested in only long-term fixes, the kind you get from connecting with others who really understand you, others who have walked in your shoes.

We hide for a long time in our secrets—that's human nature. But the end finally comes. Don's charade ended, along with his marriage, his job, and his role as a father, but with the help of a loving Higher Power, new friends, and his own willingness to do whatever is asked of him, the future has a silver lining. There is always a silver lining, and Don trusts that this will be so. In the meantime, he is spreading the word that no matter how great our losses, there is still reason for getting out of bed each morning. God isn't done with us. Every breath we take is our assurance of that. We may never be the same as we once were, but we will be what God wants us to be now.

April Suggestions for Cultivating Hope

1. Wanting to control others and the outcome of situations is typical for many of us. The practice of letting go frees us in ways we'd never have imagined. This month, keep track every day of times when you "walked away" rather than tried to control someone or some circumstance that was none of your business.

2. Choosing to be peaceful rather than argumentative is an act of letting go. Was there an argument you opted not to have recently? Describe in your notebook or journal what you did and how that felt.

3. How many times are you choosing to smile rather than react critically to a situation that you can't control anyway? Take a moment to write a few lines about how that change in your behavior feels.

4. It is said that our actions reflect love or fear. Make a chart of your behavior every day to see *where* you spend most of your time.

Love Is Letting Go of Fear.

Jerry Jampolsky founded a center in Southern California a number of years ago to help children with cancer accept their diagnosis and impending death. The center's core teaching was based on changing children's attitudes about themselves, their illness, and their possibilities for happiness. Jampolsky says that what he learned from the children about their willingness to let go of their fear and accept what remained of life with a peaceful, hopeful heart far exceeded what they learned from him.

The power of this idea, that love and the peace that envelops it is the gift we receive when we let go of our fear, changes our every experience. Most of us aren't facing imminent death at the moment, but we are no doubt troubled by situations over which we have no control, situations that may be affecting loved ones as well. Over any one of these situations, we can easily fall into a state of fear, even panic, feeling inadequate because we can't control the outcome and protect others who are being affected. We assume, at least in part, responsibility for another person's happiness or success (or failure).

What a terrible burden to feel that we must protect everyone who shares our journey; we deserve freedom from this burden. We are not meant to live each other's lives—to protect one another from the experiences that are part of our destiny—but to complement each other on this journey, as teachers and students interchangeably. We need to understand this in order to clearly see what is next on our own very specific agenda of responsibilities—responsibilities that are manageable if we keep our focus where it belongs on a daily basis.

Letting go of others—their struggles and their successes—as well as the outcomes of the myriad situations we are trying to manage in our own lives is not easy and requires daily practice. Yet letting go eventually teaches us that freedom from fear will help us come to know love and the peace that is its complement, and what both can offer us. Cultivating the hope that this is so might be considered the first step to discovering real peace in our lives. If we are experiencing fear, we are unable to appreciate the love and hope that is all around us. Likewise, when we do experience love, fear disappears. Either is available. It's the choice that's the key, and we, alone, are the choosers.

Jampolsky experienced the potential in this idea through the courage of terminally ill children. That potential is within us as well.

> *Throughout this week, try to be conscious of*
> *your attempts to control the outcome of situations,*
> *those affecting you as well as those affecting others.*
> *Make an effort to step back, seeking to let go and*
> *to remember that your focus is limited, but your*
> *chances for peace are not. We cannot be fearful*
> *and peaceful at the same time, but we can*
> *choose which one we want to be.*

In Every Conflict, Ask, "Would I Rather Be Peaceful or Right?"

Being raised by a father who insisted he was always right was exhausting. Perhaps you grew up similarly. It became my nature, even as a youngster, to fight him at every opportunity. I felt like it was my job to defend the family against his certainty that there was one way to see everything—his way. He and I battled for years while my mother looked on. We fought over politics, religion, music, and even mundane things, like which television shows were worth watching. We were on opposite sides of every issue that was raised. Even after I married and moved away, the disagreements continued. They had become habitual.

I gradually learned how to give up the fight to be right. For so many reasons, I am grateful for this. For one, my father and I were able to have a few peaceful years before he died. I had been introduced to the idea that anger of any kind is usually rooted in fear, and this allowed me to see him in a whole new way. His anger wasn't really directed at me; it was at anyone who thought differently. His insecurities simply demanded that others agree.

I was overwhelmed by the power of his fear when I interviewed him for a family-of-origin class I was taking early in my recovery. He told me that he had gone to work afraid every day of his life, afraid he would make a mistake that would cost the bank money and destroy his good reputation. I was stunned by his comment. I couldn't imagine how it must have felt to show up for work every day, afraid. And even though this conversation occurred years after his retirement, he was still that same man, still afraid and still needing to be quite certain that his way of seeing the world was the right way.

At that moment, I felt truly sad for him for the first time in my life. I could see him as he really was, not as the tyrant I had made him out to be. Fear is so debilitating. It doesn't allow for clarity of thinking. It generally doesn't allow for openness to new ideas. When fear is your constant companion, it feels safe to live in a restricted frame of mind. I am amazed at the many successes my dad actually had, considering how fearful

59

he was. He had obviously pushed himself to excel in spite of his daily struggles with fear.

The choice to be peaceful rather than right doesn't actually mean our opinions are unimportant. In fact, our particular opinions may make more sense in the larger scheme of things. Letting go of the battle is certainly far more sensible than the folly of expecting to change another person's mind. I credit Al-Anon with strengthening this resolve in me. The power of detachment, the willingness to choose to be peaceful rather than make every conversation a battleground, is freedom at its very best. There is no mystery in how this is done. It's a decision any one of us can make as often as the opportunity to disagree comes up.

> *We don't really even have to hope for a more*
> *peaceful life. It's ours just as quickly as we make*
> *the choice to want something different in our daily*
> *interactions. Remember, those who come forth*
> *provide us with opportunities for practicing peace.*

If Peace Has Eluded You, Choose Your Perspective Once Again.

Have you ever heard the phrase "I can choose peace instead of this"? Every time I hear it, it reminds me just how simple life can be. The phrase calls to mind the Al-Anon philosophy that so many have committed to over the years, a way of seeing that fosters a person's willingness to let others be, to let them be who they are, to let them make their own choices and to wander their own paths. Choosing peace over the obsession to control changes everything about a person's life. I know; I am living proof—at least much of the time.

Many of us came into the rooms of recovery absolutely insane with the need to control even the tiniest details of someone else's life. We failed miserably, of course, but that didn't stop us from trying. I, for one, wasn't quick to grasp the suggestion to *let go and let God*. I just didn't understand what it meant. I truly thought it was my "job" to make sure others did what was expected of them, or at least to remind them of their obligations. When they didn't "do their part," wasn't it a reflection on me? Or worse yet, in the case of a partner, it might mean they didn't really want to be with me. I had learned about control at the feet of my dad. He hadn't succeeded, and I didn't, either.

The freedom that comes with acknowledging that others have control over their own lives may be unfamiliar and initially feel like disinterest. However, it's the key to having a hope-filled life. Keeping our focus on others may have been how we knew we were alive, that our lives had meaning. If so, it will certainly be a new way of experiencing our lives to let go, move the focus off others, and stop living our lives through the lives of others. I seldom knew what I really thought or felt about anything before Al-Anon. What other people thought became what I thought, too. I can still remember trying to guess what my companions were thinking so if I were asked for my opinion, it wouldn't be in conflict with theirs. I vacillated between trying to control their actions and trying to be who they wanted me to be. There was no *me* at home.

Peace will never be our companion if we choose to make demands or foist our opinions, "lessons," and perspectives on others. No matter how forceful we are, we simply can't make other people do what we think is best for them or think the way we want them to; the insanity is that we keep trying anyway. They may go along with our suggestion for a while, but they will revert to how they want to live as soon as we look the other way. That's as it should be. It's their journey, after all. We will also never find peace or acceptance in trying to figure out who people want us to be. We have our own very important journey to make, and it doesn't include the care and control of someone else. That's God's work.

There will be no peace in our lives if we are waiting for others to become who we want them to be, to fulfill us in some way, to complete our dream of the perfect relationship. Continuing to "hope" for this will only make us full of doubt and feel hopeless in short order. Letting go of the need to control others is a good first step in cultivating genuine hope. The second step is experiencing gratitude for the freedom we have been given as the result of letting go.

There Is No Struggle Too Big to Relinquish.

The idea that we must join every argument *we are invited to* is ludicrous. But that's the pattern many of us have perfected after years of practice. If we intend to continue this habit, our lives will not change very much, even if we claim that we want

62

more peace on a daily basis. Being argumentative is hardly the path to inner peace. Being argumentative not only prevents our own peace, but it affects the peace of everyone around us.

Arguments are always the result of someone wanting to exert control over someone else: change another's opinion, appearance, behavior, or even the direction for his or her life. Arguments seldom, if ever, benefit anyone. The instigator may feel powerful, self-righteous, and certain of being right when he or she "wins," but in actuality, an adversary will sometimes agree to anything in the short term just to end the conflict, yet remain unconvinced and, ultimately, unchanged. Arguments truly serve no fruitful purpose, and they often escalate into situations with serious repercussions.

Why, then, are so many of us drawn into arguments? The allure of *possibly* being able to control someone else is the hook, I think. Having another person go along with our opinion, or give in to doing something the way we think it should be done, allows us a sense of false power and pride. It makes us feel secure with our own perspective and chases away the dreaded fear of possible rejection. Being committed to winning arguments at any cost is not a way to live if we're seeking to cultivate hope in our lives.

Failing to see others as our companions and our teachers— teachers who have perspectives worthy of consideration at least—cheats us from learning what they have come to teach. Let's not forget that others have appeared on our path intentionally, and we'll never know that intention if all we do is try to browbeat them into accepting our view. Their appearance is solely for the enlightenment we can offer one another. What

63

a hopeful realization this is if we allow ourselves to revel in it. Everyone who comes into our lives is present for a purpose. Everyone!

And yet, we may have a way to go before we reach this hopeful frame of mind. Hopelessness about any aspect of our lives can become as habitual as smoking or overeating. We can succumb to such hopelessness by refusing to let the suggestions of others—suggestions that might lead us out of this state—penetrate our mind-set. On the other hand, having hope that our lives can be different in any regard can begin with a tiny decision to ask, "Would you mind repeating that idea?" Moving from hopelessness to hopefulness isn't a huge step. It only seems that way if we resist seeing the other's perspective.

Today can be the first day of a new way of seeing every experience and each person who comes our way. Deciding to be enlightened rather than resistant will allow the divine plan that awaits us to unfold—now.

May

EMBRACING OUR EXPERIENCES

I accept life unconditionally . . .
Most people ask for happiness on condition.
Happiness can only be felt if you don't set any condition.
ARTHUR RUBINSTEIN

Patience Plus Trust Can Heal.

Sandy lives a peaceful life these days in small-town America, but her journey to this place and time of relative comfort has been long and arduous. For extended periods, it has been very painful, too. Unfortunately, she was prepared for the pain by a lifetime of sorrow: first as the child of affluent, alcoholic parents who were often too drunk to be attentive; then as a wife who was quickly cast aside once the vows were repeated; and finally as an employee who was verbally and emotionally abused for years on a job she couldn't afford to leave.

Sandy felt abandoned most of her life, but her first experience with actual abandonment occurred when she was five years old and hospitalized with a serious illness. She was in isolation for nearly two weeks, during which time her parents never visited her. The resulting terror that she had been forgotten forever haunted her into adulthood. For years, she doubted the accuracy of this memory because of how unspeakable it was, but her older brother confirmed it. He couldn't even recall their parents talking about her.

The disease that claimed her parents' attention, and that ultimately took their lives, didn't leave room for Sandy or her siblings even when their needs were grave. Their parents were too busy with their very active and alcoholic social lives. Fortunately, they could afford to employ a nanny, who was the primary caregiver until Sandy went away to college, a departure she had anxiously awaited.

While Sandy was at college, her mother died of pneumonia. She had passed out on the front steps of their home on a subzero night and was not discovered until morning by the neighbors. Sandy's father hadn't even noticed that she hadn't made it into the house after a night of drinking with friends. What followed was a sad funeral and a sad realization for Sandy: her mother had been abandoned much as she had been. Alcoholism is a consuming disease that leaves little room for thinking about the needs of others, and those left behind pay a heavy price.

Sandy eventually sought refuge in alcohol herself. The example her parents provided made her behavior almost second nature. And alcohol did fill the emptiness for many years. Her primary search was for security, however, and alcohol simply can't meet that need long term. In fact, as dependence on alcohol increases—as it always does for an alcoholic—escalating insecurity becomes the reality. Along with her dependence on alcohol, Sandy became dependent on male attention, too. She unconsciously hoped that men would offer the security she couldn't find with alcohol, and because she was attractive, men were easily snagged. Yet this solution was also ineffective long term because the relationships never lasted.

So Sandy went from bar to bar, partner to partner, and then settled on a marriage that met none of her needs. He had proposed, and she thought that getting married meant she would no longer be alone and searching. However, the very night of their wedding, her husband left the house and didn't return for five days, at which time he gave no explanation of his whereabouts. She was frantic and felt abandoned; the experience triggered the feeling of terror she had known as a five-year-old. For the next few years, Sandy and her husband wandered the halls of their home in virtual seclusion from one another. When the actual divorce came, it simply made their reality legal. Although Sandy moved on with her life, the wound festered for decades.

I met Sandy after her divorce and after she had quit drinking. Alcohol hadn't solved any of her problems, and she was ready for a genuine solution, which she found in Alcoholics Anonymous, a solution we shared. Over dinner, we discovered that though our paths were different in many ways, we had both sought validation from unavailable men. We provided great support for each other, and our friendship has endured ever since. Still, Sandy's journey has been fraught with painful times, difficult people, and extreme uncertainties. Were it not for the support of friends and the principles of recovery, it's doubtful she would have survived.

Sandy's job in the finance department of a state agency was anything but rewarding. Although her position was secure, her emotional circumstances at work were not. She was the constant target of fellow employees, a situation she could never discover an explanation for. Nor did she have any readily available recourse. She kept her nose in her work and struggled to handle her daily tasks, trying to ignore the constant jabs and criticism from co-workers. Her boss spent very little time in her building, so she couldn't easily turn to him. Once again, she felt alone, which she found no less painful in adulthood than she had in early childhood.

Those of us who knew Sandy well marveled at her loyalty to a job and a boss who offered little support or understanding. Because he never observed her colleagues' behavior, he thought she must be overreacting. She needed the job, the benefits, and the pension, and so she felt she had to stay. Were it not for the constant support she received through friends and Twelve Step meetings, she may not have been able to continue working in such an abusive environment. Fortunately, Sandy's boss was finally forced to spend more time at her office, where he witnessed the behavior she had endured for years. Heads rolled. Sandy was finally able to quit on her terms, with her boss's blessing and with her pension intact.

It had been a long haul and very unfair, but she learned so much. She learned that all things can be tolerated if you have the desire to let a Higher Power be a part of your life, and if you rely on that Power through all of your experiences. Sandy is the walking poster woman for the slogan "We are never given more than we, with God's help, can handle." She has been a beacon of hope to many others since she began sharing her story at meetings. She convinces her listeners that nothing has to hold you down if you walk with the presence of the God she grew to count on in the rooms of AA.

The final stage of her professional life was spent in a position where she was appreciated not only for what she knew but also for who she was. It was a joy to see Sandy finally receive the accolades she deserved. After retirement, she left the city and returned to the small town of her youth. Interestingly, she has been able to put to rest many of the painful memories from her childhood by spending time in the home where she was born, the home where her mother was left to die on the front steps, which has now become a bed and breakfast. She helps at the bed and breakfast, doing tours and sharing her good memories with the visitors. This has completed the cycle of healing for Sandy.

She has come to understand that her parents, like all of us, did the best they knew how to do. She has clarity now that her life has been leading her back to this town, back to this home, back to her past with a new understanding. And she is grateful. Even after a life that was so tragic and painful for so long, Sandy is one of the most grateful women I have known in my thirty-five years in recovery. When I think of her story, I immediately think of the poem "Footprints." It fits her life so well—God was carrying her. With absolute assurance, she tells others that they are being carried, too.

69

May Suggestions for Cultivating Hope

1. For this month, seek to notice at least one challenging experience every day that you can embrace, knowing it has brought you to a new level of understanding of your journey. Describe the experience in your notebook or journal and thank your Higher Power.

2. Reflect on the past two or three months. Do you recognize any experiences that stand out as ones you can now see had special meaning? Make a note of something you learned.

3. It is said that we are never given more than we can handle. Take note of the "hard stuff" in your current life and observe how you perceive those situations and then how you handle them.

4. All people and all experiences provide us opportunities to grow in peacefulness. At the end of each day this month, make a note of one experience and describe how it strengthened your willingness to experience peace.

~

Perception Is Not a Fact.

Another word for perception is *interpretation,* and our interpretations of events vary widely. No two people ever observe exactly the same thing. Past experiences are generally the lens through which we look at present situations. Our past experiences are very important, in fact. They help to inform the choices we make every day: not just decisions about what we are seeing but also ones that determine how we are feeling and behaving, too. However, we may have misperceived some nuances of an earlier situation because of information we weren't privy to. When this happens, we will carry our faulty perceptions—our ill-informed interpretations—with us, and these can lead to unhealthy choices.

We aren't wrong just because our perception of a situation differs from someone else's. But being aware that we all have a unique lens through which we see our world can free us from the burden of insisting that our view is the only one possible. If we all shared the same perception of events—both personal and global—there would be no conflict. But our world is assuredly not free of conflict. Siblings, couples, countries, and tribal groups have been fighting and going to war since time immemorial.

Perceptions aren't facts, and we have opportunities every day to either compromise with others when our viewpoints differ—coming to an agreement about the situation—or to quietly resort to our own "counsel," going within and asking the God of our understanding to help us see the situation from a different perspective. Either choice is a great exercise for releasing our willpower and attaining peace. Being "right" is always a matter of individual perception, and once again, there is no one right perception.

While I don't mean to come off as a strict, uncompromising proponent of conflict-free living (although I *do* like to avoid it in my own life), I do believe there is value in learning to live among those who "see" differently than we see. We can even celebrate our different perceptions because they can present unexpected opportunities to grow in willingness to allow others to be who they are, rather than who we want them to be. Every day, we gravitate toward people we need to encounter because of the lessons we are destined to share. And it's these very people—people who have perceptions important to them though different from ours—who give us the wisdom we need, just when we need it.

The next time you're in a discussion with someone you're not seeing eye to eye with, remember how very important this opportunity is. Our wisdom deepens every time we are offered a perception that's different from our own. God is present when this happens. Be grateful and hopeful that it happens often.

Perceptions aren't facts. Many times,
they have grown out of misunderstandings.
They will always serve as fodder for the ways
we need to grow. And this is a fact!

All Encounters with Others—Those We Already Know
as Well as Strangers—Are Helpful.

Is your memory bank littered with experiences that were unpleasant, or even dangerous? Although I never feared for my life, I probably should have. Had I been sober in some situations, I would have been afraid. Many times, I have been stranded in places I should never have been with people who were strangers.

As we age, the accumulation of "unsought experiences"

(not necessarily all dangerous) seems to grow; I say *unsought* because we have no concrete recollection of requesting these experiences before awakening to them. Carolyn Myss, a spiritual intuitive and author, makes a strong case for our having prearranged, *before birth,* every experience we ever have, and with particular people, too. Although this may seem implausible, it offers an explanation for situations that may otherwise be unexplainable. Of course, we remember more than the negative situations in our lives, but they are the ones that stand out for most of us.

More than three decades ago, a sponsor told me that every experience was according to God's plan for my life. Though I didn't argue, I doubted her words. I couldn't fathom that the painful years with my first husband or in my family of origin were part of the plan. Nor the sexual abuse that happened when I was young. All my sponsor said, again and again, was that there was a plan unfolding. More would be revealed, and I was to have hope.

I remain unconvinced that God actually *orders* everything that happens in our lives, but I am convinced that God is present to see us through whatever does occur. I think our egos, interacting with other people's egos, play a role in many of our daily troubles. Fortunately, God doesn't judge the ego's behavior. God simply says, "I'm here."

When the newcomers I sponsor look to me for answers or guidance about troubling events from their past or present lives, I tell them what my sponsor told me: *a plan is unfolding, and everything is right on schedule.* I tell them that every difficult experience I had strengthened my character and inspired gratitude for what I learned. As time passed, I also realized that I could survive any situation if I allowed for the grace of my Higher Power to be a part of the outcome. I assure them that what has been true for me holds true for them as well.

That's the beauty of walking among our friends in these rooms of recovery and elsewhere, too. We can remind one another of what's true, through our words or our actions. We can help others shoulder experiences that haven't yet begun to make sense and help them have hope. I am convinced this is the part God does play in our lives. We are not meant to be separate and isolated, but walking in concert with one another.

What a gift hope is. It makes the onerous tolerable,
the confusing acceptable, the hurtful forgivable.
Hope changes our hearts as it informs our minds.
Sharing the wisdom of hope with another person
is a mighty offering to both of us.

Every Experience Is an Opportunity to Live
a More Peaceful Life.

At a spirituality workshop I attended many years ago, one of the participants asked the speaker how she could possibly have a good marriage if her husband wouldn't join her on her spiritual path. I thought the speaker would say the chances weren't great. Instead, he told this woman that she was living with the best teacher she could have found. He then explained that those people who are easy to live with don't push us to strengthen our ties to God and the peaceful path He reveals.

I have thought about that workshop and that speaker perhaps hundreds of times over the years. I have also passed his wisdom on to many people who have posed that same question to me. It's natural to assume that our smooth relationships are the best ones. While these relationships may indeed be the most enjoyable and peaceful (and surely don't need to be discarded!), they may not be teaching us all that we deserve to know. I would never suggest we exchange an easy relationship for one that's more chaotic. What I am saying is that whatever relationships we find ourselves in are the right ones for now. They are teaching us what we are ready to know at the present time.

I'm relieved to finally understand that every experience I'm having is wearing my name. This truth has allowed me to accept that some rather unpleasant experiences from my past are worthy of a second look. For instance, I believe now that my first marriage, painful though it was, pushed me through the doors of graduate school. The dissolution of that marriage was necessary for the next stage of my development, which ultimately led to recovery and the work I have been doing ever since. I couldn't see this at the time, of course; I thought the bottom had fallen out of my world. Hindsight is crucial for a better understanding of so many things. I know that whatever happens in the future will be opening doors to my next key growth spurts.

Take a moment to consider some of the situations you thought you couldn't survive in your past. Can you see, now, how they fit into your current circumstances? The next stage of your development will follow suit. We are simply always in the right place at the right time. That may seem like such an absurd idea, and I hated it when I first heard it; but now it brings me a sense of relief every time I hear it. We don't have to be mystified by what's happening. God is part of the experience, and we are being led to a peaceful place of understanding if we will simply set aside our skepticism.

Attaining the peaceful life isn't beyond our capabilities. It takes willingness, period. When any experience gathers your attention, move into it, knowing that it has come calling for a reason. Know also that we are never expected to go alone into the experience. Our Companion is ready and waiting and always a mere request away. The two of us together will be at peace within whatever has presented itself.

> *We have been called to every experience*
> *that visits us today. Be peaceful.*
> *Our Higher Power is there waiting for us.*

Detaching Is an Act of Love.

Successfully "detaching" from the behavior, the opinions, and the personalities of others—not allowing any of those features to determine how we feel in a specific moment or about ourselves in general—gives us genuine hope for a life of freedom and joy. Unfortunately, we will be exposed to much that's mean and spiteful throughout our lives. Those actions are evident everywhere: at home, in the workplace, in the neighborhood. Far too often, we have been on the receiving end of harsh, uncalled-for treatment. It wasn't easy to detach from what we experienced and realize that it wasn't a reflection of who we really are. It's even harder, however, to embrace all experiences for what they can teach us. And yet, that's the suggestion I am making. From every experience, we can grow. From every experience, we will learn something that we can pass on to others, which is actually one of the main reasons for our experiencing it. Hindsight offers us this wisdom, doesn't it?

Allowing our traveling companions their own personal journeys, rather than the ones we'd like to orchestrate for them, is the ultimate act of loving detachment. Being "attached" to the emotional turmoil that troubles others—the kind of turmoil that can spill onto us—and letting it control our own emotions is the barrier to peaceful living that we have to come to grips with. While it's true that embracing all of our experiences helps us better understand our journey—our very "divine" journey—other people's highly charged experiences should not control our emotions in a negative way. On the contrary, all experiences, ours and those of others, are meant to educate and enlighten, not send us scurrying for cover.

While this is a book about hope and the promise for a more peaceful life that comes from the cultivation of hope, I know that few of us dwell in a hopeful repose all of the time. Experiences within our families and with other significant relationships often left us bereft of hope. For many, myself included, alcohol and other drugs were a constant and readily available solution for the anguish we felt. Choosing that as a solution leads to death or, if we're lucky, to an opportunity to walk through the doors of a fellowship that offers another way to perceive one's experiences. In my using days, I never knew that what I lacked was hope. My use of alcohol, other drugs, and unhealthy relationships with men had become habitual, a simple fact of my life. And I never expected to find hope when I wandered into the fellowship. Now it pervades me. My emptiness has been filled.

Hope may be viewed as a wonder drug, a drug "prescribed" by those whose mental, emotional, and physical health has improved through their cultivation of it. They sought and found the help we now seek, and to them we can look with gratitude. Our journeys are intersecting quite intentionally. The well-being we're experiencing as the result of those intersections is intentional, too.

Noticing our traveling companions is a blessing.
We walk side by side because of what we can learn and
teach each other about hope and its many promises for
our peaceful journey. Doing our part is easy. Just be
present and willing; God will do the rest.

June

CHOICES

*One cannot collect all the beautiful shells
on the beach. One can collect only a few.*
ANNE MORROW LINDBERGH

*Choosing, Once Again,
Was Her Key to Peaceful Living.*

Observing her childhood, one would never have imagined the journey Carol was destined to make. The same could be said for many of us, particularly those of us who end up in recovery programs. Her youth was spent in a small town near the Canadian border. She was the daughter of a successful physician, a man who also happened to be alcoholic—a fact unknown to her at the time. She had a privileged life—summers at the family's cottage on Lake Ontario, private boarding schools. Yet money and privilege didn't help when she was faced with the death of her father when she was sixteen, and that of her brother, who died shortly thereafter.

In her quest for answers to these losses, Carol turned to poetry and religion. She was very angry at God for taking away her two favorite people. She entered college still searching and still angry. Before her father's death, she had planned to pursue medical school, but now she feared the pressure to fill his shoes would overwhelm her. Since she loved poetry, she decided instead to major in English, with thoughts of becoming a professor.

When that didn't work out as planned, she applied to law school, where she met her first husband. After graduation, they moved to Georgetown, in Washington, D.C., when he took a position there. Three years later, she was hired as a law clerk in Philadelphia. This position eventually led to a higher-level job, a plum post that required constant travel. Most of her work was in other states, and she would be on assignment for as long as a year at a time. Her marriage didn't survive, but alcohol helped her cope with this lifestyle.

Carol's journey into full-fledged alcoholism didn't begin until she returned to Philadelphia to stay, but her drinking had certainly brought her highs and lows before then. After her alcoholism had become apparent to her colleagues, a lawyers' group confronted her and encouraged her to seek treatment. She did, and that's where she met her second husband. Shortly thereafter, she lost her job, which marked the beginning of a very long downward spiral that has only recently reversed its course.

Her second marriage produced a wonderful son, but it also resulted in years of domestic violence. Carol finally escaped the marriage, and she and her son moved to Florida, where her sister lived. It wasn't long before her ex-husband showed up in

and a lengthy sentence of probation and restitution for the property damage she caused. Carol was also diagnosed with post-traumatic stress disorder (PTSD) stemming from her abusive second marriage.

Carol, determined not to let these setbacks destroy her, eventually got the help she needed and now uses her knowledge of the law to help organizations that treat women in circumstances similar to those she survived. She is committed to giving back. Best of all, she and her son are no longer estranged. Life is looking good for Carol. That she is finally experiencing good times also benefits the women who look to her for guidance. It has been a long road for her, but her life teaches us that we always have a choice. Carol made the choice to persevere. She knows she has a wiser program now. Her service on many boards, her availability to others in the fellowship, her willingness to be a guide, or way show-er, wherever the opportunity presents itself means that her work is far from over. For that, she's grateful, and so am I.

June Suggestions for Cultivating Hope

1. How we react to any experience is a choice. Can you see when your choices aren't fostering peace? At the end of each day for the next week, record what some of your choices were and their consequences.

2. What thought have you held on to lately that caused you pain? Can you think of one to replace it with? Do this

exercise with any thought that causes negative emotions during the week.

3. Making a choice doesn't imply taking an action. When have you made a "silent" choice this week?

4. Even when our loved ones are angry, we don't have to respond with anger. When have you put this into practice lately?

Anger Is Almost Always Masking Fear.

The anger of others, whether friends, family members, or strangers, can be extremely intimidating. Depending on our own state of mind in the moment the anger erupts, we can become afraid, assume responsibility for it, try to mollify the one expressing it, stand up to it and express anger ourselves, or quietly withdraw to safer territory. All of these are common responses, but none of them is the most beneficial way to respond to whoever is angry. Certainly, none of those responses takes full advantage of the opportunity before us if we understand it for what it actually is.

Anger often signifies fear, frequently intense fear, which is generally misunderstood by the person expressing it and just as often misinterpreted by the observer of it. But once we learn that anger is usually fear in disguise, we start to see some of the dynamics of our interactions and relationships, past and present—within our families, in our marriages, with friends and colleagues at work—in a new light.

It's important to acknowledge that an undercurrent of fear that finds expression as anger in one's interactions causes harm to those who are haunted by it as well as those on the receiving end. On the national and world stage as well, history is replete with examples of how fear can turn peaceful people into unyielding tyrants seeking revenge. The power of fear is mighty and far reaching, ultimately affecting the entire human race if left unchecked. *And yet there is reason for hope in the midst of this turmoil.*

The world can begin to change. All it takes is for a single fearful, angry person to shift her perception about a situation or a person, and then make a better choice about her own behavior. The idea that one person can make such a difference may seem far-fetched, but indeed, that is how any change, large or small, begins to materialize. What this means is that every one of us, together and individually, can impact how the circumstances of the world continue to evolve. We can determine whether or not we will experience peace in our personal lives and, by our actions and example, bring about peaceful resolutions in the lives of others, near and far away.

Many will say it can't be done—there will always be cynics among us. But those who believe in the miracle of change live among us, too. Whenever any one of us recognizes someone else's anger for what it really is and responds with understanding and compassion, we all move closer to the peaceful existence that can be ours, here and now. "Nothing changes if nothing changes"; we can be the change agents who will make a difference.

It's not as difficult as it may first appear
to confront fear and anger with love and
understanding. The decision to do so is the first step.
Making this decision every morning is the second step.
Observing the success of this choice every night
is the third. Nothing will ever be the same again
when we make this a daily practice.

Our Thoughts Can Be Changed, Lessening
the Pain of Any Unexpected Experience.

This principle may seem simplistic. What about the death of a child, spouse, parent, or friend? Isn't the pain of those experiences real and palpable? Of course it is. Hurricanes, forest fires, and floods destroy homes and lives on an all-too-frequent basis, causing pain and suffering. We only have to remember the suffering caused in 2005 by Hurricane Katrina, displayed to the world by nonstop television coverage—and many continue to suffer from that disaster long after the cameras left. We watched helplessly as the 2004 Indian Ocean tsunami killed hundreds of thousands of people throughout Southeast Asia. Pain and destruction are real, whether caused by a major disaster affecting thousands or a personal trauma affecting one person or family. But with a little willingness and reliance on a Higher Power, we can try to see what has occurred from a different perspective.

86   We have a choice in how we perceive any traumatic event, whether it's of human origin or a natural disaster. We can

choose to feel betrayed by an experience, believing that what has happened is unfair, or we can say, "I may not understand the meaning of what has happened right now, but I will in time. More will be revealed." Or better yet, we can say, "I don't ever have to understand why this has happened, but a Power greater than myself can help me accept it, and in time, perhaps, just perhaps, even be grateful for it."

Making the decision to allow for an explanation to surface later, or trusting that whatever has happened fits into a much larger picture of our lives, a picture we simply aren't privy to yet, makes any situation tolerable even though we might not like it. Having hope that this is so becomes the gift we receive when we surrender our need to have a clear picture of the future. Hope becomes the balm that eases any feeling of dis-ease or quiets any fear about the next steps to take on our journey.

Indeed, our thoughts about any experience do make a difference in its impact—so much of a difference that I would go so far as to say that it's the thought that matters more than the experience itself. Let me be clear: Events that trouble us, in any way, should not be minimized, discounted, or ignored. Nor should we discount experiences that trouble our companions. Our work here is to let our actions be guided by this truth: we can survive whatever occurs if we know whom to turn to for comfort and if we offer support and compassion to others when they need it. Being the sign of hope for a traveling companion consumed by fearful thoughts may be our most important assignment. Having hope when others have none is our gift.

*Hope is the byproduct of faith that our journeys, with
all their twists and turns, are intentional. We may not
believe this every day, especially when the unwanted and
unexpected occur, but if we have surrounded ourselves
with others who share this awareness, we can help one
another remember it when needed. Our thoughts are
nothing more than an invitation to remember God.*

Having Hope Is a Choice and a Decision.

The idea of developing a more hopeful perspective on life
is more plausible when we accept that we have the personal
power, right now, to *make the choice* to be more hopeful. In
other words, hope is not entirely elusive, and never is it un-
attainable. Perhaps it seems that way at times, particularly if
we have been struggling in a dead-end job or a painful relationship that brings little joy or peace of mind. But we can
change our circumstances, or how we feel within them—even
while leaving the external circumstances unchanged—simply
by deciding to change our minds. The power that comes from
this very important exercise is always available to us.

We have all been in the company of others who see the
bright side of every situation, no matter how difficult. Perhaps
we admire that quality in them; sometimes we may envy it;
and, depending on our frame of mind, we may even resent
it. The lesson for us here is that what someone else can do,
we can do, too. It's just possible that the person standing before us with the positive perspective has been sent to us as a

guide, as an example of another way to see the world as full of opportunities, where we may see problems. Remember, our messengers are everywhere. They will seek us out—we cannot hide from them.

This principle offers great comfort if we make the effort to understand it and practice it. We make many decisions daily and are constantly offered opportunities for making choices. Every meal we eat, every book we read, every idea we share, every plan we make with friends is based on an unconscious or a conscious decision. Making choices is second nature to us. Many of them are made with little thought, but they are choices nonetheless. Should I call a friend even though I am tired? Should I eat this dessert even though I'm on a diet? Seeing these "habits" as opportunities for the creation of hope in our lives is a simple step, actually, but it's one we have to be willing to take.

The idea that hope can be developed out of any circumstance in our lives is exhilarating. While it may seem unimaginable at first, we can follow the example of those who have done it. Our periods of hopelessness, while overwhelming at the time, can be observed as teaching us something we need to learn. For example, I became closer to God on each occasion I felt hopeless. I sought God's help in prayer and meditation, and I felt comforted and convinced, once again, that I had not been forgotten. My search for an answer seemed to draw others closer to me. There is always a silver lining to hopelessness if we become willing to open our hearts to people who are trying to show us another way to see. There is always another way to see what is happening.

Being privy to the successes of and the sharing from others
is a great gift, a great opportunity for us to realize that
our own successes await us. What is available to others is
available to us, too. God doesn't pick and choose who will
know peace, who will be free of pain, who will receive
the blessings of a life well lived. We are all gifted equally.
We can count on this and have hope for our future.

A Little Willingness Is the First Step
to Full-Fledged Hope.

It's doubtful that anyone shows up at a support group full of hope and promise, clicking his heels with joy. Many, in fact, come afraid, miserable beyond measure, and certain that an even worse tomorrow is about to befall them. Few people seek any kind of help unless they feel some element of desperation. How glorious it is that wherever we are, in whatever group we find ourselves, we can offer a beacon of hope, a beacon of light, to all the seekers who come. In fact, because we have already found our way (or are finding it) to a life relatively free of fear, we can be the "light" for others. And our light doesn't shine just at particular gatherings. That's the really fortunate result of what we are learning. Wherever we go, everywhere we travel, we take who we are becoming with us.

The choice to take a different fork in the road has always been an option. Any one of us could have remained stuck in old patterns and unworkable relationships, full of self-pity and troubled by a host of other counterproductive thoughts and

behaviors. We know many who didn't follow our ex
who took the different fork, the one leading to a life
manent despair. Some are no longer alive as a consequence.
But the nudge we received was felt, and now we are nudging
others to choose as we have. It's a special opportunity we have
signed up for.

Backsliding is a reality, though, and we have to be both
vigilant and willing to make the choice for this new path, this
new vision, every day. That's not a bad thing. On the contrary,
making it anew each day is like saying hello to God every
morning. Our conscious contact with the God of our understanding, made on a daily basis, keeps the light of hope alive
in us. Why? Because we no longer feel alone as soon as we
have made the contact. God always answers our call. Hope is
maintained if we do our part. And when we fail to make "the
call," we get a second or third chance. God waits for us. We
can restore our hope by doing the next right thing. We only
need to get quiet and listen.

Our forgetting occasionally may actually offer an important lesson we need that we can, in turn, give to others. By
showing our traveling companions that hope is never lost forever, we give them courage to stay on the path, to stick with the
"program," and to trust that where they have ended up is exactly where they have been heading for many years. When they
stumble—and they will stumble—all is not lost. Hope waits
for them. Their job is simply to pick themselves up and believe
once again that what seems impossible is really God's invitation
for them to trust that He can do what we can't do alone.

It takes very little for us to find the peace we desire and

deserve. Peace follows in the footsteps of quiet prayer, a willingness to experience a result different from the one we're used to, and the longing to be hope-filled rather than full of dread that the worst is just around the corner. What we find in any moment is exactly what we are looking for. What kind of "now" do you really want?

Deciding to be hopeful will influence every experience we encounter. That doesn't mean troubling circumstances will never happen; rather, it means that we will face them with an open heart and a faith that God is present to help us handle them.

July

PERSPECTIVE

To have a crisis, and act upon it, is one thing.
To dwell in perpetual crisis is another.
BARBARA GRIZZUTI HARRISON

◦⌒◦

God Had a Plan I Could Not Have Foretold.
He Always Does.

I chose the month of July as the right place to share my own story of hope for two reasons. First, I was born in July seven decades ago. It doesn't seem possible that I took my first breath that long ago. And I am utterly amazed to be sitting here, in this chair, at this computer, telling you about my journey. This is not how I had imagined my life would unfold. I am surely grateful that God had a better plan for me than the one I had imagined. Second, that's where this month's topic, *perspective,* fits in. The shift in my perspective about the possibilities that exist for all of us has been miraculous. It's said that a miracle is nothing more than a shift in perspective, a shift that God helps us make. I have found this to be true ever since I made the decision to acknowledge *His presence,* a presence I had resisted knowing for more than thirty years.

But let me begin at the beginning. I was an extremely fearful child in a family of four children. I think all of us were afraid, actually, including my mom—afraid of the angry outbursts that often, yet unpredictably, erupted after my dad came home from work each day. It was seldom clear what he was angry about. Sometimes a bike would be in the driveway or the newspaper was askew or one of our many cats startled him, but often he just came in the house tense, with lips pursed, and I could sense it was best to avoid him. I never rushed home from my friends' houses after school, expecting a warm hug and freshly baked cookies on the kitchen counter. My mom seemed to be always on pins and needles, and she didn't easily mother us the way some of my friends' mothers did them.

There wasn't any extreme physical violence in our house, but the yelling, the swearing, and the silent treatments kept me constantly vigilant and uneasy. Although I did get my share of light spankings for minor infractions, the real beating I got was emotional. My unrelenting anxiety over the rage in our house made me easy prey for the relief I discovered, quite by accident, that came from alcohol. It happened at a wedding reception when I was thirteen. No one was watching as I poured some whiskey in a glass of Coke. I don't know what possessed me to do it. It was there, and I just did it. And then, wow! I had never felt so warm inside and so totally at peace. It's almost frightening to recall as vividly as I am right now how it completely transformed that moment. From that day until I took my last drink twenty-three years later, alcohol was my friend, my comforter, my security blanket. It changed my outlook on life. It was my constant companion.

Along with alcohol, I soon craved the attention of boys and, as I got older, the companionship of men to complete me. Predictably, both dependencies took their toll, but it took years before I was willing or able to acknowledge where my journey had taken me. One of the realities of recovery, at least from my perspective, is that our journey has always been perfect and "on time," moving us in the right direction no matter how many times we meander off course. I meandered many times. I pushed against many doors marked "do not enter." But I made it to where God had intended anyway, as I believe we all do. There are no words for God's grace. It simply is bestowed on us, unbidden.

My first marriage was alcoholic from the start. We met at college, in geology class. He was smart and cute and had a red Buick convertible. We discovered we both loved to drink and party and cut classes. He eventually flunked out. I was placed on social probation for drinking after hours in his fraternity. We got married in my senior year, against my better judgment and my parents' wishes—alcohol had decided for me. He eventually got back into school, and then I supported us while he philandered his way through a master's degree. We moved to Minnesota, and by then our marriage had deteriorated to the point that I was actually praying that he would drop out of my life through death or an accident or something I couldn't be blamed for—but not the way he ultimately did. He found another woman and left me. I was devastated, not because he was gone but because I was humiliated. In my alcoholic mind, the invitation to drink even more couldn't have been clearer, and I didn't hesitate in accepting it.

One of the saving graces in my life back then was that I had followed him into graduate school, teaching at the university and, much to my amazement, earning straight A's. These grades served as a much-needed positive reward in a life that was otherwise at loose ends. I never knew what to expect next. I just kept showing up and so did the truly miraculous A's, along with the men and the alcohol. As insane as this sounds, I think my surprising success was all part of God's plan. I was not a scholar by any means; I had been an average student as an undergraduate. It was like my life was on its own trajectory and someone else was living it, wearing my skin—someone much smarter and more clever than me.

When I was introduced to the Promises of the program of Alcoholics Anonymous, I saw a glimmer of how God had been doing for me what I could not have done for myself. But before getting to that first meeting, I had many close calls with death. Driving drunk against traffic down one-way streets, racing on back streets to escape the "stranger" who was chasing me, and scoring unknown drugs from street-corner dealers were all ordinary events in my life. Yet I somehow continued to perform in school and as an instructor at the university. Indeed, God was present. My life was surely in the hands of a Power greater than myself.

Many of us who finally "make it" have a history of dodging the proverbial buses; my journey isn't unusual in that regard. Finding gratitude for "the buses" and the other close calls takes willingness. Gratefully, I have a lot of that. I have now been on this sober path for nearly thirty-five years, and I am still amazed at how God's plan has played out in my life.

I am amazed that I found my way home many a cold night from unfamiliar neighborhoods, after having spent the evening with people I didn't know, in bars where I was the lone woman. I had a protector; of that I am certain.

Even after getting sober, my struggles weren't over. About a year into recovery, I hit a new bottom, one that shook me to my core. I became terrified of leaving my apartment. I didn't show up to teach or attend classes. I made no calls and didn't answer the phone. I had never felt such an overwhelming sense of fear. A dark cloud had completely enveloped me, and I was certain nothing would ever change. One day, I sat in my kitchen and prepared to take my life (an idea I had flirted with many times, even in my youth) by turning on the gas after stuffing towels around the windows; then there came a loud knock at my door. I ignored it at first, but the knock was persistent, and a woman's voice called out my name. I didn't want the neighbors to hear her, so I reluctantly opened it, and my life again changed.

Pat was her name. She hurried through the door, almost pushing me to the side. She was obviously on a mission, one I couldn't fathom. She said we had an appointment to discuss my finances. At the time, I lived month to month and was baffled that I would have arranged such a meeting. I had never seen her before. She, in turn, was baffled I had forgotten the appointment. She pulled out her engagement book to show me that my name was recorded there. She could sense I was troubled and asked me what was wrong. I told her about the depression and the fear. Her next words, "I am envious of you—you are on the precipice of a new spiritual plane," offered

97

me the hope I had been so lacking. I didn't really understand what she meant, but I could feel the comfort in her voice.

We sat at the kitchen table, and she told me her own story of depression and free-floating anxiety and what she had learned about their meaning. She gave my malady a name: chemicalization. She said my old ideas didn't want me to let them go so I could make room for a new spiritual understanding that was waiting for me. Like a naughty child, they were fighting me at every turn. Her words carried the ring of truth, and her demeanor comforted me. I felt lifted and hopeful, and the darkness receded. I felt transformed.

Pat left, nearly as abruptly as she came, and I never saw her again. I quietly put the towels away and reached for the phone. I left the confines of my apartment for the first time in days and knew I could make it now. That was more than three decades ago, but the memory is as vivid as if it had only just happened. Who was this woman? How did she find me? Who sent her? These are questions I have ruminated about for years. All I know for sure is that she came, I listened, and my life was changed forever. God does send us angels; I'm certain of this. My life is proof.

I had another very clear demonstration of receiving help from God two years later. I was waiting for the final approval on my Ph.D. dissertation. My orals were scheduled, but there had been one holdout on my committee. I had called him many times. He seemed to be avoiding me. Finally, we sat down across the desk from one another. His words rocked my reality: "This must be entirely rewritten." I am not sure how I maintained composure, but I asked if he'd go through it with me so I could understand his objections. He said yes, and here's where it got interesting. For three-and-a-half hours, we went through three hundred pages of work. He posed questions that I didn't actually hear, and I responded with words I also didn't hear. It was like an out-of-body experience. I watched and was amazed at what I observed. When we reached the end, he looked at me, smiled, and said, "I approve your work. See you at the oral."

I walked out of his office and rushed to the phone to call my second husband. "I don't know what just happened, but I think God showed up again." Sometimes I honestly wonder if I just imagined this experience. How could it have really happened? And then I am reminded of the Big Book's promise: God, indeed, does for us what we can't do for ourselves. I am comfortable now in believing that if we get out of the way, *and only if we get out of the way,* God can do His work.

Since that time, my life has run relatively smoothly. I have had no mysterious interceptions, nor have I needed a quiet voice to answer questions posed to me. But I have been blessed by many unexpected opportunities as a writer and speaker that can only be the result of God's invitation, since they had not previously been on my radar screen. According to my plan, I was destined for a life on the edge with people who loved the edge, too. But there was another outcome more befitting. Even though I didn't seek it out, it found me. That's the miracle of life. Our part is simply to say yes when the invitation comes. God does the planning and then helps with the follow-through. It's really not all that difficult once you get the hang of it. How glad I am to know now that I, too, am a member of God's infinite community, and I am committed to carrying the message, *God's message,* to all who will listen.

July Suggestions for Cultivating Hope

1. Perspective is all-powerful. Seeking to see the glass half full will allow a different day to unfold. List the times (be specific) you practice this idea for the next few days.

2. Asking God for help in seeing our experiences and our companions differently guarantees it will happen. Share your experience with how this worked each evening for one week.

3. Can you recall a recent situation when you changed your perspective about a person or an experience? Make a note of it for future reference.

4. Being in charge of how you see the world around you is exhilarating. List some specific times this coming week when you took advantage of seeing only the good in a person you encountered. How did it change the rest of the day's experiences?

Choice Determines What We See and How We Feel.

When a good friend shared this idea about choice with me a number of years ago, I was surprised and thought she was being rather unkind. Couldn't she see the way I was being treated by a mutual acquaintance, a woman we both had known for many years? I had experienced too many put-downs by this particular person, and I was certain I was undeserving of every one of them. I so wanted my friend to take sides, to join with me and say that "our friend" was out of line—cruel, in fact. Instead, she said I could look at the woman's actions and hear her words another way, if I so chose.

These words contain wisdom: making another choice about how we see the behavior or hear the words of others is an extremely helpful and powerful action available at every turn. It's one that will make a significant difference in how a day unfolds. Hearing someone's words as criticism and having those words determine who we are in that moment is giving away our spiritual power. When we let other people's rudeness—or decision to simply ignore us—define us, we have chosen to let them serve as our Higher Power, rather than relying on the true Power who has always been present in our lives when sought. Making another choice about how to interpret our experiences is empowering, and it's what our Higher Power is waiting for us to do.

Unfortunately, I spent most of the first four decades of my life letting other people's behavior define me. I just couldn't grasp that what they did and said revealed only how they felt about themselves. I got my first glimmer of what I had been doing nearly forty years ago, when I read a story in which a prominent Jesuit priest talked about frequently strolling with a friend to buy a newspaper from a vendor. The vendor was repeatedly rude, and yet the priest's friend was always kind and even tipped him. Perplexed, the clergyman finally asked, "Why are you so nice? He doesn't deserve it." His friend said, "Why should I let him decide what kind of day I am going to

101

have?" When I read that, the waters parted. I was astounded by his explanation. *Choosing how to see* a person or an event makes the difference in how we feel.

Had I been able to take advantage of this wisdom right away, I'd have saved many years of painful feelings of inadequacy; but we become ready, often slowly, to make the changes that have been waiting for us. I simply wasn't ready to absorb this information in a way that would inform my life. Thankfully, that is no longer the case. The changes waited for me as they wait for all of us. But we all know many who still struggle in the same way I struggled. It's not easy to take responsibility for how we see other people's actions. It's not easy to say there is another choice I can make, one that will allow the other person to be human and even flawed. It's not easy to release others from our judgment and experience the freedom this gives us. Our negative interpretations hold us hostage just as much as they prevent the other person from having the dignity they deserve.

> *Choose again. That's the suggestion here.*
> *It's a simple idea, and it frees everyone.*
> *It's the choice God would have us make.*
> *Help (and hope!) are awaiting us.*

We Cannot Directly Change the World, but
We Can Change How We Choose to See It.

102 This principle isn't a simple one. Believing that it is our task to change the world around us isn't uncommon to people

who want to be accountable and responsible citizens. But over time, I have come to believe that changing how we think comes first. Our behavior changes next, and the world then, *and only then,* reflects those changes. It's clear we have work to do; there is much in the world that needs changing. However, changing how we think—the first task—isn't an easy one. Our mind-set has become habitual, and it takes concentrated willingness and effort to even consider that there is another way to perceive the world around us. Even so, we *can* do it.

The impact individuals can have on the world has been demonstrated throughout history by many powerful people. Think of Eleanor Roosevelt, Martin Luther King Jr., Robert Kennedy, Gandhi (and I would add people like Bill Wilson and Betty Ford for the work they did for alcoholics)—the list goes on. We continue to feel the impact from changes that minds such as theirs had the courage to make. These people were often expressing ideas that were unpopular at the time, and they encountered widespread resistance. In fact, three of them were assassinated for their views, and yet the ideas they cherished have lived on.

We are all being called to look closely at the world and to ask ourselves, "Is this the world I want to live in? The world I want the next generation to inherit?" If it's not, we need to be willing to do the next right thing to change it. For most of us, the next right thing might be to change our minds so we can see the potential for a different world. There's a spiritual teaching that says we always see what we want to see. It goes on to say that if we want a "different picture," we must project one. I used to think that taking responsibility for the picture

103

that gets projected was to deny reality. Now I am grateful that I am seeing what I have chosen to see. Becoming accountable for the world "out there" helps me see how easily my thoughts lead me to places I don't really want to go.

It's a very hopeful assignment to be in charge of the world we see. Working to make this a more peaceful, loving world is a worthy task for any day. And it begins, for each one of us, by seeking to see the people we encounter as children of God, just like ourselves—looking for understanding, peace, forgiveness, and always for love. We can be the giver of each of these things. Being willing to take up this charge is the contribution that will, in concert with others, make the world a better place for our children. The world will be what we want it to be. The power to make this so is ours.

Waking up to the opportunities that come with being responsible for our minds, our behaviors, and our actions promises to make this day an exciting one that will positively affect the life of everyone we connect with. Again, the change is ours to make. Let's go for it!

A Miracle Is a Shift in Perception.

As children, many of us who were raised Christian thought miracles were limited to those special things Jesus was said to have done, like feeding the multitudes with a few loaves of bread and a handful of fish, walking on water, and healing the sick on the spot. Perhaps we thought those performances seemed a bit unlikely, but the Sunday school teacher didn't leave much room for doubt. I don't remember if I was convinced, but I do know I didn't spend much time thinking about the "works" of Jesus when I was a kid. Sunday school was fun, and that's where my friends were. If Jesus was there, too, fine.

Then in high school, I began to doubt the existence of God, and in college I quit believing in God altogether. My friends were nonbelievers, too, and it seemed cool at the time. Our worldview was dictated by the agnostic philosophers and poets we were learning about. How silly those years seem now, but we had to be where we were in order to end up where we are now.

Some years later, while in graduate school, I quietly came to believe in the possibility of something "larger than myself." I say "quietly" because I was sure my friends would scoff. I was studying American Indian culture, and what I learned about the concept of a sustaining Creator, common across many tribal traditions, gave me food for thought. I could see how that belief system had comforted many men and women, even as they were being massacred by a system that demanded their lands and the relinquishment of their way of life. My own life at the time was filled with angst, and I began to think that believing in some kind of God might be helpful for me, too. And I developed hope.

My journey then led me into the Twelve Step programs that have continued to be my mainstay for thirty-five years. Accepting the presence of a God of my understanding was like a warm comforter, a wave of hope, on a very cold night. I still feel that kind of comfort when I think of God. I begin my day with God, I close it with God, and I have made a practice of thinking of God throughout the day when I am feeling agitated. This practice has allowed me to be hopeful and at peace, even in the midst of a stormy encounter. Giving up a thought that isn't helpful, and instead making room for God, changes everything.

One of the most significant ideas I have been introduced to on my spiritual journey is that being willing to change my perception of a person or about a situation that troubles me is the true definition of a miracle. The willingness to "see differently" allows a new awareness to emerge, and this new awareness lifts my spirit. We can hold only one thought at a time. Shifting from an attack thought—and any negative judgment is an attack thought—to a loving thought brings peace to one's mind and a softness to one's heart. What a nice way to experience life. This has become *the miracle* I seek daily.

> *There is no magic in experiencing a miracle. It comes as easily and as often as your decision to see a person or a situation in a more loving or a more forgiving way. Try it.*

It Only Takes a Tiny Seed of Hope to Experience a Different Life.

Sowing tiny seeds, a ritual that farmers experience each spring, is the beginning of the life forms that will sustain them and many other families for the coming year. The miracle that a tiny, unassuming seed becomes an ear of corn, a bean, a radish, a potato, or a carrot is all the evidence we need to believe that our own tiny seed of hope can also mature and feed us in ways we hadn't imagined.

While this sounds reasonable, it's not always easy to translate what is true in the cycle of crop production to our own troubled existence. But possessing a hopeful perspective is powerful and life changing, every bit as miraculous as the reconstitution of a small yellow seed into a sturdy stalk of corn. In our mental and spiritual lives, the process is the same. A significant transformation can take place if a seed—whether it's a physical seed or a thought or idea—is properly nourished. The farmer prays for rain after spreading fertilizer and then watches the corn seeds sprout; we nurture the idea that being willing to set aside our disbelief that God does, indeed, have the perfect outcome for us will blossom into a spiritual transformation that brings sustaining hope.

Laying aside our disbelief takes courage, however. We have grown accustomed to disbelief. We've come to believe it's simply who we are. Disbelief can be like an old slipper lovingly worn at the end of a long day. We're not sure we want our lives to change. Even when we are saddled with despair and worry over our uncertain futures, we have adjusted to this uncertainty. Having a more perfect and certain outcome, one that pleases God, might not please us. That's our fear, and that's the kernel for our resistance.

We have to be open to a different life before one can materialize. Then, we have to listen to the still, small voice within, the one that inspires hope that we can do whatever it seems we are being called to do. We have all been called to do something special in this life. That's an undeniable fact. And if we aren't at peace doing whatever our current job or daily routine is, it's likely because we aren't doing what God has designated as "our work." Making the decision to open our minds and hearts to the direction we are assuredly going to receive, perhaps have already been receiving, means we have to cultivate hope for accepting the message. We may also need a bit more hope for the willingness to start down a new path, if that's what's suggested.

Allowing hope to change our perspective can be one of the most beneficial responses we ever make. Hope can open our minds like no other resource. It can become a habit, too. We have all honed many unproductive habits over the years; maybe it's time to give our attention to one that has a major payoff. Hope will open the door to the transformation we deserve, even when we aren't sure we want it. Fortunately, we don't have to cultivate it in isolation. God will offer the helping hand we need.

The perspective we currently honor may have become
timeworn and, though comforting in its familiarity,
not necessarily fitting for the circumstances of today.
Changing it, however, doesn't come easily. This is
where the cultivation of hope can play a major role.
With hope, nothing *has to stay the same. Do we*
want something different? Hope is the way.

August

LEARNING PARTNERS

Two may talk together under the same roof
for many years, yet never really meet.
MARY CATHERWOOD

❧

Vision Is More Than Mere Eyesight.

My husband and I met Monty while I was researching a book about the elderly; I wanted to know how they live with hope and grace in a world that often ignores them. Monty's story came to my attention through a book by Dana Steward called *A Fine Age*. Steward was a woman from Arkansas who had been interested in older artisans who lived in her state, and I was immediately captured by her brief biography of Monty. I made plans to meet him so that I could learn more about him and the spirit he embodied to live a full life, even though he was dealing with severe macular degeneration.

Amazingly, when I contacted him, he didn't hesitate to say we were welcome to visit him in his Arkansas home. Even more amazingly, when we arrived a few weeks later, he greeted us as though we were old friends. The first thing I noticed, of course, was his exceedingly thick glasses. The brief biography had mentioned he was a painter with very poor eyesight, but I wasn't prepared to meet a man who was nearly blind. Monty was very stately, quite tall and thin, dapper in dress, with a full head of white wavy hair. He was well into his eighties but still spry, still animated, still loving life.

As he showed us around his house—more by memory than by sight, I was sure—he pointed to the many photographs on the walls of him and his wife as well as photos of him receiving awards from renowned international scientists and Washington politicians. Monty was revered as a leading expert on growing rice. He had a Ph.D. from the University of Minnesota and spent many years in China, helping farmers perfect their methods.

In the photos, his wife, whom he spoke about with such affection and longing, appeared to be as small as he was tall. She was also an artist and had won many awards for her work. He couldn't have been prouder. Her landscapes hung everywhere, and he missed her terribly. She had died a few years before, but her legacy lay in her suggestion that her husband take up painting when he retired. He was slow to do it, he said, because it would be hard not to measure his efforts against her star-quality work. He eventually took the plunge after much pleading, and the two of them painted, side by side, until she died.

Many of their paintings had been done from the porch of the small log cabin they shared outside of town. It was a place that held many special memories for Monty, a place he didn't get to very often anymore, and my husband and I were touched when he asked if we would like to see it for ourselves. Even with his failing eyesight, he was able to give us clear directions, as he had made many trips there over the years. When we started up the long, winding road to the cabin, I could almost hear his breathing relax as we neared the place where he felt so close to his wife. His actions gave us permission to feel close to her, too.

We walked up to the unlocked front door and let ourselves in. As in their home, her paintings hung everywhere; only here, his work hung alongside hers. What a joy to our eyes to be privy to work that meant so much to him. He suggested we help ourselves to a soda from the refrigerator; then we sat down on the front porch to take in the view. His porch overlooked a valley of wildflowers and tall pines. The birds were chirping everywhere. We sat in silence for a time, and then I asked Monty to tell me more about himself and what brought real joy to his life.

He began by saying the memory of his wife gave him the most joy. His daughter and grandchildren were a close second. When I asked him about the work he had done for so many years, and the acclaim he had received, he said all of that paled in comparison to the thrill it was to paint every day. Just as his wife had painted every day when she was alive, he, too, made painting a part of his daily life now. At first I doubted his words, but then I saw the smile on his face. The passion he felt for having released this creative spirit was evident in every crease of his gentle smile.

After sitting for an hour or more on the porch, much of it in silence, we got back in the car and returned to Monty's house. Here we sat in his sunroom, and he shared more about what his life was like now, on a daily basis: After breakfast and a short chat with his daughter on the phone, he went to the easel and began to paint, mostly from memory, the sights he had seen at the side of his wife. He said his heart soared every time he picked up the paintbrush. It was the one time he didn't feel the angst of her passing, as he was certain she was guiding his brush across the page. Every day his routine was the same, and it kept him peaceful.

Monty was and is a wonderful example of hope-filled spirit. Everything about his life was as dark as the rooms in his house when his vision faded away after his wife died. With his daughter's encouragement and his own willingness to recognize his wife's wishes, he was able to continue the journey they had begun together when he picked up his paintbrush again a few months after her death. Although he still missed her, he no longer felt she was distant. Rather, he knew she was as close as his memory, and this knowledge served him in a way that his eyes no longer could.

While we sat, ruminating about his words, Monty got up and walked quite purposefully to the easel. He picked up his brush, adjusted his magnifying glass over his right eye, turned his head slightly to the left, and began to paint. He didn't speak, but he was smiling. He seemed to be already in communication with his wife. Perhaps he was telling her about us, I thought. We wondered if we should quietly leave and so rose to depart when he said, "Wait, please, I have something for you." With that, he took the painting from the easel and handed it to us.

We were dumbstruck. It was a winter scene, breathtakingly beautiful. It could have been a Minnesota winter day, obviously painted from memory—his and his wife's, no doubt,

112

since he had lived in Arkansas for so many years now. We thanked him for his time, his wisdom, the gift of seeing his cabin, his demonstration of courage, and the picture that still hangs in our own log cabin in Indiana. As we drove away from Monty's home, we realized that possessing the spirit of hope to go on after the seemingly worst has happened is what makes someone like Monty a guide for the rest of us. It's not easy to pick up the pieces at any age, but to do so when your own life is coming to a close reveals a vision that's far keener than ordinary eyesight.

August Suggestions for Cultivating Hope

1. Look carefully at all the people you interact with over the next few days. Take a moment at the end of each day and write down some reasons you think certain people crossed your path.

2. The people who trigger anger in us are teaching us the most, some would say. If this is true, what have you recently learned and how has your worldview changed?

3. Someone who disagrees with you is giving you an opportunity to broaden your mind or make the choice to remain quiet. Have you experienced either response recently? Write how it felt in your notebook or journal.

4. Hope is contagious. Make a note of every time you perceive it in others for even a day. How does that recognition change you? Share your feelings about this in your notebook or journal.

*Every Experience Is Offering the Next "Right" Lesson
and the Right Partner to Learn It With.*

This idea can be exceedingly comforting. The past is not a
pretty sight for many of us who finally wander into the rooms
of recovery. As I shared in my story, my early life was replete
with experiences that were ugly, oftentimes dangerous, and,
according to others, on the edge of insanity far too often. But
I survived them all, and now that story has, on occasion, been
helpful to others who have come to me for guidance. I eventually developed hope, hope that my life could be as sane as the
lives of those men and women who carried their message to
the recovery meetings I attended. The hope I developed from
listening to others is what I now freely offer to the "wanderers" who come my way, until they have the capacity to create
hope for themselves.

When we are yet unable to ignite hope for our own lives,
it's a blessing to observe how it has played out in the lives of
others; those examples serve us well. Having hope is akin to
finding food when you are starving. It allows you not only to
continue living, but also to have the strength to do what had
seemed impossible only days or perhaps even moments before.
Hope is a powerful elixir. Without it, lives remain unchanged
and that which is ours to do remains undone.

And what an elixir hope is when it bears fruit in the belief
that, no matter what experience seems to be catching our attention, it is truly the next necessary thing for us. The corollary
to this principle is that the person who "carries" the experience
to us is part of the lesson we have been waiting for. We can
trust that we have been fully prepared for the lesson and the

"carrier." Nothing comes to us that we aren't ready for. We may want to resist a particular experience or lesson, but this is where hope can play a role. Knowing that what has come to us is *by design* diminishes our fear and releases in us the further hope we need to fulfill the responsibility that has come calling.

We may have seen it played out in our own lives: a lost job opens the door to a better one or a broken relationship prepares us to better appreciate a more rewarding one down the road. But other experiences can be harder to assimilate and process: the death of a loved one, the abuse of a child, an entire community devastated by a flood or hurricane. It's not my intent to argue that seeing such tragedies as necessary and part of a divine plan is logical or easy; I only offer this as a possibility for how to accept the "unacceptable."

We simply don't know the design for anyone else's life. We don't know the specifics of anyone's journey. That's between each person and the Creator. What can be known is that we can all gather around the people in need who cross our path, offering our love and support. We can pray for their loved ones to remain strong and faith-filled. We can pass on hope to those who have no capacity for feeling it in the moment. And we can know that every time we experience hope for anyone, it strengthens it in all of us.

> *It's a relief knowing that what comes every day*
> *is part of a larger plan. It takes the worry*
> *out of the day and makes room for the hope*
> *that's necessary to move forward.*

115

Our Learning Partners Have
Been Divinely Selected.

Those we travel these roads with have made their trek to us because they need us and what we know as much as we need them and the lessons they offer. This idea has been discussed in earlier essays, but it's worth further examination. Knowing that every person is specific to our education means we don't have to be afraid of the experiences before us. We have been guided to each experience, and we will be led through it, too. I have often heard it said that God never brings us to an experience without also promising to carry us through it.

I was encouraged to see the truth in this idea many years ago. A wise sponsor suggested that I had nothing to lose by believing my life was unfolding as it should. I would always be at the right place at the right time, facing the next right opportunity, she said. How right she was. Even when the path got rocky—and there were many times it did—I hung on to her suggestion that I was ready for whatever transpired.

The experience of my professor challenging my Ph.D. dissertation and me being led through the process of convincing him of its validity offers a particularly potent example of God answering my call even though I wasn't aware I had made one.

I remember reading the book *Illusions,* by Richard Bach, very early in my recovery. At the time, I was scared and confused by the changes occurring in my life. I also doubted that my life had any real purpose. But I was willing to be comforted by any reasonable suggestion, and I found it on the back cover of that wonderful little book. It said, and I paraphrase: *if you are reading this now, that means you are still alive and your purpose has yet to be fulfilled.* That simple statement gave me the lift I was so desperate for at the time, and it is still a great reminder. I am still alive, and so are you; therefore, we still have work to complete.

Knowing that we still have important work to do is rather exciting. That work will continue until our journey finally detours and takes us to the last, peaceful stage. Until then, our most important purpose may be to help those around us develop the hope they currently lack. Some researchers now believe that hope can be taught, that people can be shown how to build on their existing strengths rather than focus on what they lack. We can, in our role as guides, help others discover the hope we have already found. This may well be why those others have appeared. What a worthy purpose to have been set before us.

> *Knowing that we can "teach" hopefulness by*
> *demonstrating for others how we've focused*
> *on a strength and then emphasized it*
> *gives each experience the value it deserves.*

Every Person Is a Potential Learning Partner.

I recently met someone at a friend's home whom I took an instant dislike to. Everything about the man got under my skin. He was loud; he didn't listen to others when they spoke; he seemed particularly dismissive of women; he was very judgmental, from my perception; and it seemed we had nothing in

117

common. Then I heard him mention he was in recovery. What a difference that piece of information made to me! I wondered why I was so quick to dismiss him and then just as quickly forgive him his apparent flaws when I found out we shared the most important of all my values.

This gave me a lot of food for thought over the next few days. I had heard all the clichés: "you spot it, you got it" and "everyone is a mirror of yourself." I did recognize some of my own characteristics in this man, particularly those that I abhorred, but I still wondered what allowed me to instantly see him differently when I found out we were both in recovery. I haven't completely sorted this out, but I do think having the willingness to set aside my judgments when I want to means I can set them aside even when I don't want to. They have not become hardened in concrete, but are merely hovering over my shoulders until I throw them off. The decision to do so is always as close as my next thought.

What I most realized from this meeting is that this man served as a great learning partner for me—that every person who crosses our path is a potential learning partner. I was willing to cast him aside after judging him and concluding that he had nothing to offer me. In fact, his very presence reminded me once again that every person is "in my face" for a reason, and there's a lesson to be learned, if not now, later.

Nothing that happens is by chance. Every person who wanders into our lives has been called to that moment in time. Isn't this a hopeful concept? Doesn't it change every past situation that you hated? Doesn't it shine a new light on every person you meet that you aren't immediately drawn to? It means we can live free of dread. We can anticipate all that may happen in every tomorrow with joy.

Most of us experience times of hopelessness. I have had my share, many even after I was in recovery. You recall my story about Pat, the woman who knocked on my door as I was preparing to take my life. In hindsight, that experience and others have demonstrated that when I experienced the least hope, God was still trying very hard to reach me. And finally the message got through. I can promise you, the same will be true for you. We are never left to handle our hopelessness alone. If you are in a situation that seems uncomfortable, ask yourself, "Is there something here for me to learn?"

> *God is always trying to get our attention through the*
> *messengers He sends our way. Hope is really a way of*
> *life—it's God in action. There's nothing mysterious*
> *about it; we just need to trust that whoever comes to us*
> *is the next learning partner we are ready for.*

Discover Freedom by Changing Places
with Your Perceived Adversary.

Far too many of our encounters with other people have an element of tension in them. We see people as adversaries, oftentimes with little or no provocation. Our own insecurities usually prompt this response. The downside of our reaction is that we are held hostage by it. We can't see our lives as they really are or make decisions with any clarity if we are allowing ourselves to be held prisoner by our judgments against anyone, either friend or imagined foe. It's possible to alter this pattern of behavior, however. We can see everyone who crosses our path as invited guests to the "party" we are hosting.

The idea that we can adopt this perspective may seem far-fetched, but it's not. Emotionally, it's far healthier to see the people around us as necessary for our development than as "out to get us" in some way. Choosing the former viewpoint promises to make our lives more hopeful, too. Seeing everyone journeying across our path as a purposeful companion, rather than a dreaded enemy, will foster our growth. Staying stuck is always an option, and that's exactly what's in store for us if we hold ourselves hostage by being unfairly judgmental and suspicious. Too many of us have done that for far too long.

Shifting our perspective from seeing others as adversaries to seeing them as teachers takes little more than the willingness to take a deep breath and then choose to look again. We will see who and what we want to see, always. Inviting the God of our understanding to look with us at the people and the situations that have presented themselves gives us the benefit of seeing more clearly who and what really stands before us.

That fearful part of our self, our protective ego, holds fast to the power it wields. And because our associates are sometimes difficult to get along with, it's easy to give in to that fear and assume the worst about them. However, if we choose to see and live this way, on a daily basis, we will undoubtedly be miserable.

120

There is another very simple remedy. Dare to see ourselves from *the other person's perspective,* even for a moment. Walking in the shoes of our imagined adversary can be enlightening. Doing so almost always frees us from the judgment we had been holding. Being willing to see everyone who walks beside us as trying to do their best, just like ourselves, shifts our perception quite effortlessly. And isn't that what we really want—lives without tension, without the constant unease that accompanies judgment of our traveling companions? We certainly make our lives more stressful than they need to be. In fact, we would have little or no stress if we didn't distort the world that stands before us.

> *No one holds us hostage but ourselves—no one.*
> *There are no adversaries on our path, but we can create*
> *them. There are teachers, and there are students. We all*
> *take on both roles. We can see every person and interpret*
> *every event with hopeful hearts rather than judgment.*
> *The choice is ours, and the hope-filled choice is easy to see.*

September

LOVE VERSUS FEAR

*One of the attributes of love . . . is to bring
harmony and order out of chaos.*
MOLLY HASKELL

*God Orchestrates Our Lives. We Need Only to Stay
Out of His Way and Listen to His Guidance.*

Lacie was born in a small village in upstate New York,
the youngest of nine children. It was a proud family where
the adults worked hard all week and drank hard on the week-
end, yet Sundays were reserved for church. She remembers
all of the families in this small town as loyal, hardworking,
and churchgoing. The pews in both black churches were
filled every Sunday. Indeed, many of the worshippers were her
relatives.

In many ways, it was an ideal setting. Everyone in the
village looked after everyone else's children. "Your 'aunts and
uncles' were everywhere," she said with a chuckle. No one was
afraid of offering a bit of discipline if it was called for. The early
years were joyful ones for Lacie, but when she was six, her
mother unexpectedly died. It was a terrible blow, but she was

well cared for by her older siblings and many aunties who took over her mother's role. She never left the house uncombed, disheveled, or unfed.

Her father quickly remarried. Although she liked her stepmom and felt loved, life just wasn't the same. Her home now included two stepsiblings, and Lacie's own brothers and sisters were beginning to leave home for college and places unknown to her. She began looking outside her home for the comfort she craved, and indeed, she found it—with drugs and men. Alcohol and weed became her companions of choice; men ran a close third.

In spite of making bad personal choices, Lacie was still a good student and had the opportunity to travel to Washington, D.C., to meet President Ronald Reagan. The entire trip and experience left an indelible mark on her, one that she now refers to as "the hand of God." Yet her life was clearly getting off track. Others began telling her so, but she didn't listen. When you are in the throes of addiction, you can't hear the messages that are telling you to slow down, to make a better choice. Lacie finished high school but decided to put off college. She struggled with feelings of depression, which she thought were lessened with alcohol and drug use. Her choices brought her the security, albeit false security, she thought she needed. She was very good at listening to only what she wanted to hear, as is true for all addicts. And her "messengers" were telling her to hang out in the bars, use drugs, and lead a life of abandon. Because her companions were easily found—they were on every street corner—she stayed on the journey with them. Her path had been full of promise at one time—a path not unlike the one her siblings and friends had taken—but that time was past, for now.

Lacie traveled the low life quite comfortably for some time. But she eventually hit some rough spots and low points, including one in which she left her baby daughter alone in a car when she went to buy drugs on a lonely, dark street—a memory that still haunts her. She is exceedingly grateful that nothing happened to her or her daughter that night. She acknowledges that the hand of God was always present in her life.

Lacie's lowest point, as well as her turning point, came when she was arrested for shoplifting. Although she knew that shoplifting was wrong, she felt it was a necessity in her life. When the arresting officer asked if she used drugs, she didn't deny it. It simply hadn't occurred to her that drug use was illegal—everyone she knew used drugs.

A judge gave her the choice between treatment or jail. With an eight-month-old daughter, it didn't take her long to decide. She left her daughter safely in the arms of her parents and entered a new phase of her life. Fortunately, the treatment took. At 286 pounds, she walked in and met her first counselor, a tiny woman who knew any game Lacie thought she might play. Lacie's intimidation tactics—tactics she had used successfully for years as a way to cover up the fear that consumed her within—wouldn't work here, with this counselor or these peers. What a blessing.

One of the key messages Lacie heard shortly after her arrival was that few of the women present at that moment would be sober the following year. Lacie wanted to be one of the women who made it. She wanted a different life and was there to claim it.

After leaving the treatment facility, Lacie moved to a half-way house. Here, she learned the importance of focusing on herself instead of others. She also learned the most important lesson of all: *to stay in her shoes*. This meant, don't plan the rest of your life, or the next month, or even the week ahead right now. Today is what counts. Living one day at a time is what God has given us, and that's all we need right now, to do what needs to be done to stay sober. Lacie is certain of the fruits of this message and freely shares it with her colleagues now and the many young women who look to her for guidance.

Even though Lacie easily absorbed the message about addiction, she didn't have an easy road to travel in some respects. Yet she did, with work, perseverance, and the help of God, have many successes: She lost 110 pounds and got her first good job. Then she came home from work one day to find her boyfriend and her roommate high. This unexpected blow could have thrown Lacie off course, but by now, she had forged a relationship with the God of her understanding that was far stronger than any relationship she had with a roommate or a boyfriend.

After another bad roommate experience, Lacie decided to live by herself. She never felt alone anymore since she had turned her life and her will over to a loving God. Her gratitude, by this stage of her recovery, made her resilient enough to attempt many new things. She pursued jobs in unfamiliar fields because she knew the God she had learned to rely on would always do for her what she couldn't figure out. And she was right. Promotions and many opportunities followed. One of them opened the door to working in the addiction field.

But God had a plan, and He called her to move on. She went to Atlanta to visit her brother and discovered that was where she needed to be. How right that decision was. She is confident—and I became confident, too, while listening to her story—that had she not gone when first "inspired," God would have come calling again, and again, if necessary. That's how God works, after all.

Lacie met her future husband and the father of her son in Atlanta, and eventually they started a cleaning business. This is where the mystery of how God works in our lives next unfolds. Even though the cleaning business was successful and they had many clients, one family in particular became crucial to the rest of her story. This family was white, wealthy, and troubled in many ways. Lacie's preparation as a counselor enabled her to help them in numerous ways. It also helped to open her eyes to the many other troubled people around her in Atlanta, people in shelters and those who were on the streets. In her heart, Lacie knew she had to do something.

She called the wealthy man for whom she had cleaned and asked to meet with him. That visit resulted in a $5,000 check, a business plan, and a full-blown desire to open a place to house women who were struggling with their addictions as Lacie had struggled. Mary Hall Freedom House was born on that day more than ten years ago. Since that time, more than three thousand women have been helped, along with their children. Today, there are seven different housing components all working to make the dreams of women come true.

Lacie embodies all that is good and true about the spiritual principles we are privy to, no matter what spiritual path we are on. She knows that her future is God's business, rather than hers, and she will go as directed.

I have never doubted that God orchestrated all of my life, once I got into the fellowship. But spending time with someone like Lacie confirms that God always was there and always will be there. Our job is to stay out of His way and to listen to the guidance. Had Lacie chosen to stay on the path she was on as a drug addict, she might never have arrived at her current situation. That's always the choice our free will gives us. God will always wait in the wings for us to change our mind, however. And isn't that a loving, hopeful thought?

The angels are hovering over you and me and Lacie. Let's allow them to comfort us this day.

September Suggestions for Cultivating Hope

1. For one day, keep a tally and categorize all the responses you hear others making as either loving or reflecting fear. What conclusion can you draw?

2. People appeal for help in so many ways. Describe the ways you observe these appeals on a day you set aside for this activity.

3. For several minutes each day this week, pay attention to your thoughts and notice any patterns of fearful or judgmental thinking. Are you content with them? If not, do you think you can replace these thoughts when they come

up again with loving thoughts? Share your thoughts in your notebook or journal.

4. The internal feeling of love can be encouraged by a decision. Practice feeling and expressing love to your companions for the next week and keep track of the effects, both on you and them.

If It Isn't Love, It's Usually Fear.

I was first introduced to this idea as I timidly began my spiritual quest in the 1970s. This concept broadened my perspective on how to experience life and the many relationships I seemed to be "inviting along for the ride." Becoming a student of different spiritual ideas offered me a deeper layer of understanding about every life that was touching mine, an understanding that complemented my early journey in AA and Al-Anon.

Interpreting the actions of others, or trying to, had long been my primary focus, even in childhood. This meant I was never primarily engaged in my *own* life—I was an extension of other people and their lives. If they were happy, so was I. If they noticed me, I was relieved and felt important. If they were mad or sad or distant, I felt responsible and unworthy. My experience in this way of being and seeing is not unique. I have met many others who struggle just as I did to find a more peaceful, less *attached* way to live. Fortunately, we can now be guides for each other. In fact, that's why we are on each other's path; we have sought each other out whether we realized it or not.

Coming to see that anyone's actions or words are an expression of either love or fear—*their love or their fear*—and not

129

related to me or anyone else, has been a relief and a remarkable awareness, and yet, one that I still sometimes forget. There can be no lasting peace in any person's life if her every mood or action is tied directly to the moods and actions of others. Even though I've been speaking about my own personal experience here, I hold that the same dynamic is true for individuals, families, communities, and even nations as we see this principle played out in diplomacy and understanding on the one hand and division and conflict on the other.

Decisions are made every day based on the misinterpretations of other people's actions. Knowing this is the first step to perceiving differently, which opens the door to behaving differently, too. If we are prone to being fearful, our actions will be defensive or aggressive, or perhaps we withdraw from a relationship altogether. But we can make another choice. Having hope that change can happen in our own lives fosters the belief that change can happen anywhere. As I've said many times, we are the guides, the way show-ers. It's not an accident that we are sharing this information at this time. We have work to do.

*For the next few days, try to be conscious of
how fear, your own or another's, is playing out.
Seek signs of love, too. Both expressions are evident
everywhere. Meeting an expression of fear with
understanding, compassion, or love will have an
impact that goes far beyond that moment.
There is joy in knowing we have work to do
that's worthy, one moment at a time.*

We Reduce Fear and Open the Door to Peaceful Solutions When We See Others as "Chosen" Companions.

Do you monitor what you are saying and how you are feeling in conversations? If we are truly attentive to what's going on and being said during even ordinary encounters with others, we'll be surprised to discover how often fear, which wears many masks, initiates and colors our actions and reactions toward others. For many, it's the common position we revert to. It's so familiar that it almost seems to call to us, like a cat meowing to be fed.

Our fearful self clings to the power it holds over us even though it keeps us distant from God. However, reclaiming our lives and inviting our Higher Power to help us make all decisions—those concerning the present as well as those affecting our future—will ensure our peace of mind. Being in communion with the God of our understanding is the key to lives of hope rather than living in constant uncertainty about what might transpire next—and that's what living in fear promises.

It may seem simplistic to define our decisions and our actions as always reflecting love or fear. We want to think we are more complicated than that, perhaps. However, believing that every comment, thought, or action can be placed in one of those two "camps" is a choice we can make, and doing so brings tremendous relief. It actually makes it easier to monitor ourselves. And I've discovered that we can't change what we aren't monitoring. Change may not be on your agenda today, but if you are seeking peaceful relationships, and most of us are, some change will probably be called for eventually.

We may need to compromise, learn to let go, forgive, and be willing to make other choices; this will be easier if we have charted our myriad responses, whether verbal or silent, into these two simple categories.

Being inspired to live from a place of love on a daily basis, rather than letting fear be in charge, isn't beyond the realm of possibility. Nor is it probable that we can make the decision only once to live "in a state of loving expression." We vacillate between love and fear because we are human and because the ego, the creator of our fear-based responses, doesn't release us easily. But making a daily decision to be loving is a simple exercise, one we can do with the first cup of coffee—and the second one, too, if fear again comes calling. Choosing again and again to be in a loving state rather than a fearful place is the key to realizing authentic hope and peace of mind.

When I was younger, I assumed fear had its own life, that it was its own entity that had inviolate power over me. I lived with constant anxiety about the actions and, most commonly, the anticipated rejections of others. My home life, where anger was the common denominator, fed my fears. Even though I eventually understood that fear fostered the anger in my home, it was many years before that realization eased the inner feelings of uncertainty that haunted me. I am no longer haunted. I live in hope now.

Living in a state of hope is guaranteed
every time you choose to express love rather
than let fear determine your actions.
Some call this a miracle. I call it deserved.

Are You Allowing Hope to Create the Potential for Change?

Most successful people have an attitude of hope. They aren't necessarily gifted with greater intelligence than others or have more than their share of luck. However, unlike people who remain fearfully stuck in old ideas—often held hostage by even the simplest of problems, never scaling very far up the ladder of success—people who do advance often possess a strong measure of willingness to believe that wherever they are, God has a message for them that will move them farther along their path. Trusting that they will go where God wants them to contribute next is the key that allows them to relinquish their fear.

It's so easy to get trapped by fear—fear about leaving a job, or a familiar neighborhood or city; fear about learning something new; fear about upsetting a relationship—the list is endless. We can get comfy even in situations that are actually detrimental, not because they are meeting our needs but because we are afraid to give up what we know. The trust we need to develop to move on requires love, particularly for ourselves. It doesn't mean loving the unknown itself, which is never easy; it does mean trusting in our readiness to cultivate hope and the belief that all is well, that each fearful situation presents us with the opportunity to develop our ability to build that trust. There is a definite rhythm within the evolution of our lives; nothing is happening out of sequence. We do have the power to disrupt the sequence, however, by choosing to stay stuck in fear.

We all hear about people who have succeeded against all odds, such as those who overcame disabilities—whether public figures like Franklin Delano Roosevelt and Helen Keller or the hometown amputee veteran who learned not only to walk but to run. What allows these people not to give up on themselves? It's usually because they live in an atmosphere of hope nestled in love rather than fear. And when they don't feel it for themselves, others continue to sustain that atmosphere of love until hope is renewed. Love or fear. I believe that these two emotions give birth to every opinion and every response we make. Which one we choose may answer the nagging question of why some of us survive hardships and continue to thrive and others don't.

Once again, categorizing responses made by others on our path as being initiated by love or fear enables us to more quickly take control of our own reactions. Recognizing that responding lovingly—regardless of the situation or the words thrown at us—is unfailingly the appropriate response and the one that reflects God's response. It will make life so much easier, more hopeful, and definitely more peaceful. Living from this perspective also decreases the number of decisions we have to make. Love is the one true perspective, the one right reaction, that reflects God's wish for us. Put more simply, to know God's love is the one right prayer for every situation.

We don't ever have to wonder what our next right
thought should be when we view all actions as symptoms
of either the love or fear that's being felt. The guesswork
is removed. Being hopeful for ourselves and one another
is the remedy for all situations, large or small.
It's the only solution that will promote peace.

October

TWO VOICES IN OUR MINDS VIE FOR ATTENTION

*Even a happy life cannot be without
a measure of darkness.*

CARL JUNG

*With God as Our Guide, All Things Are Survivable
and Perhaps Even Understandable.*

Jose was a child when he came across the U.S.–Mexican border with his dad and his uncle. He didn't know where they were going. He only knew that he was to stay quiet and follow directions; he sensed that what they were doing was dangerous. Their first stop was in Texas, where he worked alongside his dad and uncle for a season, picking fruits and vegetables. They eventually settled in Florida, and that's where our paths crossed, more than four decades later.

As a youngster, Jose learned English quickly and soon became an interpreter for his dad and his uncle, which made him feel important as well as independent. The rest of his family eventually joined them in Florida and, in time, were naturalized. Jose is grateful for many things that have happened in his life since childhood, but he has fought many demons, too. And that's really where this story of hope takes us next.

In the United States, Jose got a good education but also learned a lot of things he would have been better off not learning, especially how to drink and score drugs. Unfortunately, he was a quick study at both. Alcohol grasped him with a stranglehold and took him to places he had never counted on going. He also put his loved ones, including his wife, through hell.

Although he managed to avoid prison time, he had many run-ins with the law for disorderly conduct. Overnights in jail were commonplace. Fortunately, he had a forgiving boss, one who understood the power of alcohol himself, so Jose didn't lose his job and worked for the same company for many years. Yet as the addiction progressed, his life spiraled downward. He eventually became homeless, living in and out of Dumpsters. During that time, his family no longer recognized him, nor wanted to. Nor did he want them to see him in this state. Amazingly, he did manage to work a few days a week and eventually get off the streets.

His journey into recovery began after meeting a man, a co-worker, who saw something in him that he hadn't seen in himself. It started with a simple invitation to share a cup of coffee after work. Jose had no reason not to, and in that moment, his miracle began.

Over coffee, the two men talked about the struggles of life, how expectations are often unmet, how families often need more from us than we can give. Then Jose's new friend asked the question that marked the turning point in his life: Did he think he had a problem with alcohol? Jose was both relieved by the question and afraid of answering it. He wasn't sure what the man wanted to hear, and he didn't want to jeopardize his job. He didn't answer at first, and then the man made it easy. He asked, "Would you like to go to an Alcoholics Anonymous meeting with me?" Jose went and has not looked back. His new friend became his first sponsor. That question and that cup of coffee were the start of the next chapter of his life. And Jose's "book" is still being written.

Jose is, by some standards, a poster child for recovery. He has not relapsed since he entered the program. This doesn't mean his journey has been easy. After reconnecting with his family, one of his children was struck and killed by a drunk driver. Fortunately, Jose had the willingness to believe that with God as our guide, all things are survivable and perhaps, in time, understandable.

Jose and his family were, of course, devastated by the death; his wife and other children cried for revenge. Jose did, too, initially. And he wanted to drink—he wanted to drink his rage, anguish, and powerlessness away. Fortunately, the only action he took was what the program told him to do in such situations: He called his sponsor, who reminded him that a drink would only make the situation worse. His sponsor also told him that he needed to forgive the person who caused his son's death.

Although Jose wasn't ready to hear such advice at that point, there is no time line on forgiveness. Whenever we are ready to open our hearts is the right time for the change that forgiveness ushers into our lives. That time came soon enough. As part of Jose's service to the AA fellowship, he "carried the message" of hope to a nearby prison. On one such visit, he "miraculously" met up with the man who had killed his son. I put quotation marks around the word *miraculously* because I believe that all things that happen in our lives are part of divine order, and what we consider miracles are just part of God's plan. This "coincidence" was certainly part of the divine tapestry being woven for Jose. He couldn't bring himself to say hello the first time he saw the man, but he knew his assignment was being shown to him.

He talked to his sponsor about the experience. He prayed and sought guidance, and prayed some more. The next time he visited the prison, he saw the man again and nodded to him. He found it hard to contain himself. He wanted to yell at the man for the life he took from Jose and his family. He wanted to strike the man until he suffered as Jose had suffered. He wasn't sure the man even recognized him, in spite of the many times they had sat in the same courtroom. Their eyes met now, but no words were exchanged. The man did come to the meeting that Jose was leading, however. He sat quietly and listened, and when it was over, he darted out.

On his next visit, Jose was ready to break his silence. With the help of his sponsor, he had prepared what he would say, but the man didn't come to the meeting this time. However, as Jose was leaving the cell block, the man hurried up to him and said hello. That wasn't all he said. He asked Jose for forgiveness. The two men stood face to face, with tears streaming down their cheeks, and after a moment, Jose reached out to give the man a hug. Their embrace closed the gap and healed both hearts. It allowed two men to begin again living the life God had intended for them.

The man's name was Jake, and on Jose's next visit, Jake was at the meeting. After it was over, he came forward and asked Jose if he would be his AA sponsor. Jose didn't hesitate. He was quick to say yes and even quicker to thank his Higher Power for allowing him the willingness to let the past be gone and to look to each day with an expectant heart, knowing that whatever God has in store will be the next right thing for him. Jose continues to be Jake's sponsor. The two intertwined stories are excellent reminders that God is always doing for us what we can't do for ourselves.

When I met Jose in the fellowship, he had already celebrated nearly twenty years of sobriety. His story was captivating, one of the most grace-filled and hopeful I had ever heard. It reminded me that hopefulness is a mind-set. Some circumstances make being hopeful more difficult. However, when any one of us revisits the past even briefly, we can see where the hand of God was present. Jose's story is a case in point. The tragic loss of his son served to introduce two men who had work to do together. Some wise voices say that the act of forgiveness is our most important work in this life. Jose's relationship with Jake offers us an example and hope that we, too, will be able to step up to the plate when the time comes.

October Suggestions for Cultivating Hope

1. Does your ego or self-will ever lead you astray? In your notebook or journal, describe some examples of when you

observe this happening in the week ahead. How can you counter this?

2. Are you aware of "the Quiet Voice within"? For one week, try listening for it before you begin the day's activities. Write down what you hear. If it's only silence, write that down, too, and see if you can decipher what the silence means. How does it make you feel?

3. It is said that this Quiet Voice will tell you what you need to know. At the end of each day for a week, write down what you think that was.

4. This Quiet Voice is a voice for forgiveness. Have you practiced forgiveness this week? How did it feel? Write about the experience.

The Ego Can Mislead Us.

According to a well-known spiritual path, there are two voices in our minds calling to us: One belongs to the ego, and it's loud, persistent, argumentative, instinctively fearful. It insists on being right and seldom encourages harmonious interactions with others unless there's something to be gained. In fact, it's often certain that other people wish us ill. The other voice is its opposite. It is calm, quiet, and loving. This voice sees the holiness of others and encourages us to seek a peaceful resolution to disagreements. It's obvious which voice we should listen to. However, we seem prone to listen to the ego, mostly out of habit, allowing it to determine what we "see," which then determines what we think and say. We'll

142

never experience the peace of God's holy presence if the ego's voice is the only one we honor. Yet since it's the loudest, we have to clear away a space in our minds for the quieter voice to claim.

We can shift which voice we listen to—a move that will change every aspect of our lives—but doing so requires that we really *want* to feel different. Even though we have developed a habit of listening to the louder voice—and indeed the ego is relentless—we can always choose to breathe deeply and switch gears. We can experience a very different life. Many have done it; we see them everywhere. We hear their peaceful words and know that, though their egos may still live in their minds, their egos don't control all of their actions. We are drawn to such people, and we can become like them.

In recent years, I have become very selective about which voice I give my attention to. The years I've spent on a spiritual path have made the difference, yet the ego has not quit trying to get my attention. Sometimes it succeeds, but I know how much better I feel when I simply "observe it" and let it go. I experience too much pain when the ego has control of my mind. I don't want to *live* there anymore. Choosing to let the ego's attempt to get your attention slide right by will make you feel reborn.

What do these two voices have to do with cultivating hope? Having hope about any aspect of our lives—whether it's resolving a conflict at home or at work, or something much more mundane like wondering how to make the right choice in how we interact with a salesperson when shopping for a new car—will be nearly impossible if the ego is in charge. The

143

ego is too intent on having its own way to leave much space for cultivating a hopeful outlook. Hope for a peaceful outcome to any experience lies in the quiet spaces of our minds, and it's where our "better self" lives.

If we really want to live more peacefully with others, we only have to open our minds to the "quieter voice." Nurturing our hope is the key to seeing and behaving differently *with everyone*. Until we make a practice of listening to the quieter voice, we will not make the changes we are here to experience. We will not reflect the hope that helps others, too.

Hope is the result of discovering we can *be different.*
It's as available as our next breath. Breathe deeply now
and move forward in your life. It's waiting for you.

We Have Two Voices in Our Minds. Only One Knows "the Way" to Love's Expression.

Perhaps you had not thought of the pull to say and do unkind things to others, friends or strangers alike, as the work of the ego's voice in your mind. But knowing this fact can be very helpful as we move along our spiritual path. We are seldom in doubt about which voice is speaking if we listen to the words being said and the directions being given. In recovery group rooms, we hear others refer to E-G-O as Edging God Out. That is a simple but accurate description of the work the ego is intent on doing. Unfortunately, some of us are too willing, sometimes even eager, to let it take charge of how we show up in an experience.

We have to ask why we listen to this voice when it pits us against our friends on so many occasions. The only explanation that makes sense is that our fear that they have more, or look better, or are smarter, or are about to leave us behind propels us to verbally attack them, in hopes of diminishing their well-being in order to build ourselves—our *egos*—up. Fear is a mighty motivator, yet we always have another choice. We can seek to hear the Spirit Guide speaking to us in our quieter voice, and Love, which is always mightier than fear, will come to our aid. Fear may seem more readily available to us, but that's because we simply haven't turned to Love as often as we could. Old habits die hard.

So much would change if we made a better choice about which voice to rely on. This idea has been mentioned often throughout this book because that simple choice has the potential to change the details of how we see, think, and act. Every change we make (or don't make) affects the travelers sharing our journey. It's a simple decision, actually, that we don't intentionally make often enough. Fortunately, we are surrounded by people who, on occasion, do listen to their Spirit Guide, and we reap the benefit. We are also surrounded by those who continue to listen to their egos. We read about them in the newspapers daily and hear their stories on nightly news.

One thing is certain: it takes only one person listening to the Spirit for a wave of hope to wash over a situation, and everyone who is touched by the situation passes that feeling of hope on to others. The wave ultimately turns the tide of experience for multitudes. No one remains dry when the water of hope floods our souls. Becoming a part of the change that affects everyone alive is a profound responsibility. And yet, it's quite easily handled when we have turned to the power of our Spirit Guide, our Higher Power, our *quieter voice* for inspiration.

Everywhere we see evidence of ego in action. Deciding to be part of a movement that demonstrates Spirit in action is a mighty and worthy commitment, and this movement can begin with a single person. *Peace begins with me* is the refrain in a lovely song. Listening to the quieter, kinder voice allows us to be the example others need to experience.

> *Being the right kind of example for others is not a onetime decision, and then you're done. It's a decision that can be made as many times a day as is necessary. The beneficiaries are all around us.*

Our Quieter Voice Within Tells Us All We Need to Know.

The need to know God's will, particularly when it comes to major decisions, is paramount in many of our lives. We get pulled in conflicting directions, especially if we are surrounded by people who think they know what's best for everyone. It's easy to get trapped into trying to please those we care about, yet significant decisions about our lives shouldn't be based on either the whims or even the "educated" guesses of others. While some offer suggestions based on personal experiences that can be valuable, and we may indeed end up doing what they suggest, we are still better served if we rely on our own

146

counsel with the inner voice of Spirit, who truly does have an unbiased opinion of what's best for us. Having hope for the right outcome or knowing the right decision to make will always be offered from this quieter voice.

There is a certain thrill in knowing that we can always access God's will directly by taking a few moments to sit quietly in the stillness; this knowledge enlarges our capacity for hope. It's by accessing that space that the still, small voice is heard. While some claim that they primarily hear God's message through other people, either in conversation or in books— and God does speak to us in countless ways—that Quiet Voice within the stillness that's at the core of each of us gives us the steadiest and surest support and guidance. If the message isn't at first detectable, listen awhile longer. Besides, sitting quietly is usually beneficial in itself.

For many of us (especially Westerners), the practice of quiet meditation may not be very comfortable. It takes a willingness to sit through the many distractions that claim attention in our minds. No matter what kind of meditation is practiced—whether it's focusing our minds on a single word or thought, watching our breathing, or just turning in to our interior spaces—distractions are common to all "listeners." However, letting these distracting thoughts, images, or sounds slide right through our minds like sand through a sieve makes room for the real message we are waiting for. Our Quiet Voice will wait for us to be attentive.

There may be times when we have to wait awhile to hear the guidance we are seeking, but more will always be revealed. We will always know what we need to know when the time is right. That is a promise we can count on in this uncertain world. And cultivating the hope to hear that message is what invites it.

Earlier, I talked about the two voices vying for our attention. One is loud and oftentimes argumentative and generally resistant to what the other people sharing our path may be offering us. That voice seldom recommends the peaceful path to any decision. And it doesn't easily leave us alone—we have to *want* to move away from it. We have to want to let it go and instead give our attention to the quieter messenger. Just knowing that we do have a sane, loving messenger in our minds is comforting, isn't it? It waits for us, always.

> *Cultivating hope that we can be instructed by a*
> *sane and loving inner voice is all that stands between*
> *us and the guidance we deserve. The power of hope*
> *coupled with the willingness to be still is the way to*
> *discover all that we are ready to know.*

To Experience Peace, Be Open to the Hopeful Voice That Waits Quietly in Our Minds.

Choosing to listen to the suggestions of the quieter voice in our minds is not so easy, which is why I've explored this theme from so many perspectives. Doing so has had the end result of deepening my ability to heed this voice, which has helped me be more thoughtful and loving to others. We must be both willing and strong enough to ignore the other voice— our ego, our self-will—which is loud, persistent, and hard to ignore. Occasionally it's relentless, in fact, so perseverance is necessary if we want to have the peace of mind that allows us to demonstrate peace and hope to others. This quieter voice is synonymous with peace and hope. The louder voice, on the other hand, is synonymous with fear and control. Once we understand that we *have* a choice, the one to turn our attention to is obvious—except for those people who choose to live on the edge and make others miserable while doing so.

We have many role models in our midst every day, men and women who seem to be directed by the quieter, more hopeful voice. Have you ever wondered if their decision to listen to this voice has been easier than it has been for us? We see these people everywhere, and not necessarily at church, temple, or mosque. They may be friends or family members; we may encounter them in the aisles of the grocery store or at work; or even public figures appearing on television may demonstrate a kindness and calmness that we think can only come from listening to and heeding a Power greater than themselves.

The other, louder voice in our minds never completely vanishes. Because we are human, we will always continue to hear the voice of the ego, and that includes the people we look up to as role models of peace and serenity. Maybe our role models listen more intently to the quieter voice because of the payback they have received over the years. We will experience a similar reward every time we make this choice, too: the wonderful gift of a hopeful mind. If we but listen to the voice for peace, we can count on this gift with as much certainty as the sun rising every morning in the east. And like others who have had this experience, you will likely select it more frequently as your life becomes quieter and more full of love.

149

I have pondered long and hard why we are faced with making this decision between two voices. I don't know if I'll ever know for sure, but it seems to me that it's as if God is saying, "It's up to you to decide the life you want." We have the freedom to choose what we will experience, what we will know, what we will show others, the ways in which we will grow and change. We can be the example of hope that will inspire others to make that choice, or we can be miserable listening to the voice that pushes us to be disagreeable and unhappy at every turn, and spreading that unhappiness and contention to others. Both avenues have well-worn paths. But no matter how far it may seem we've gone down the path of fear and discontent, or how many times we choose that path, we can choose peace once again. That's the really fortunate thing about our experience: there's always another opportunity just around the corner.

I am reminded of the movie character Forrest Gump.
He was led by his heart and seemed to have only one
voice present in his mind. This made him gentle, kind,
and thoughtful, even when others were not being kind
to him. He saw past the attacks of others. We could
all follow his example. It's not that we shouldn't stand
up for ourselves, but choosing to do so softly and with
understanding and a desire for peace is the key.
That's the voice for hope calling to us.

FORGIVENESS

*A man that studieth revenge
keep his own wounds green.*
FRANCIS BACON

Survival in Spite of Extreme Odds.

When both parents are alcoholic, your chances of inheriting the disease are pretty high. And when one of the two parents is also severely mentally ill and both physically and emotionally abusive, the journey you travel can be treacherous. This was the case for Mac. He lived in a household where the viciousness of his alcohol- and drug-addled mother was almost unfathomable. His dad lived in a state of extreme denial coupled with the ill effects of his own near-constant intoxication, a condition that had existed ever since he returned from the Second World War. Mac's story is the stuff of fiction, but it was true—every memory of it. Every unforgotten memory.

I heard portions of Mac's story over a number of years and then asked to hear the whole story in one sitting. It wasn't easy to listen to it. The trauma inflicted on Mac when he was a child was so horrendous, I wondered how he managed to even sustain the will to live. But the human spirit is strong. That's the only answer one can be certain of after hearing a story like Mac's. Actually, all of the stories in this book illustrate the power of the human spirit that cannot be destroyed. They all describe how, against all odds, people survive—and most even thrive—after a time.

Mac had two sisters, one older and one younger, but most often they were spared from the physical abuse he suffered at the hands of his mother. While at school, he tried to hide the resulting bruises under long-sleeved shirts, long pants, and hats. When his injuries were noted by school officials, he made excuses, but they nonetheless saw what was happening and called in his parents—for which Mac paid dearly at home. Even so, his parents were never officially charged with abuse.

Mac prayed every day to be left alone, but he was seldom able to escape his mother's anger, which followed her nightly drinking. His father turned a deaf ear and tuned out, with the help of alcohol and his own painful memories. There was no solace at home for Mac. Ever.

Mac ended up in the hospital more than once with broken ribs, multiple bruises and lacerations, and on one occasion, internal bleeding after his mother stomped on his abdomen during a terrible outburst. The physical violence he endured as a child continues to affect his health even today. He has suffered hernias, debilitating migraines, and intense depression for decades. Yet he has survived and now shares his story so others will know that they, too, can survive even the most bleak of experiences.

Unfortunately, the abuse Mac suffered extended beyond

his mother's actions. He was also sexually assaulted by his uncle and his cousin for two years, starting when he was in the fifth grade. While the rest of his family prepared for Sunday dinner upstairs, he was raped by these two men in the basement of his aunt and uncle's home.

Mac was prescribed pain medications at around this time in response to his incessant crying and vomiting. Although the medications made his life bearable for a time, at least relieving some of his physical pain, he quickly became addicted to them. The meds did not help with his emotional pain, which has haunted him for decades.

Mac sought the help of a youth minister when he was in the sixth grade. Unfortunately, the minister didn't really understand the gravity of Mac's situation and contacted his parents about his concerns. They responded by punishing Mac severely. Right before Mac entered the seventh grade, he and both his sisters suffered a horrible beating from his mother, who was arrested for attempted murder. Although she was never punished for her actions, Mac was never hit again.

Mac's indomitable spirit helped him survive the next few years. He made it to college, but he had become addicted to alcohol and other drugs, which is partly why he floundered and flunked out numerous times. His confusion about life in general and what his own life in particular was supposed to "look like" pushed him to choose the ministry as a vocation. He eventually got his degree and began working with alcoholics—an ironic choice considering his denial of his own addiction.

For a number of years, Mac lived in this state of denial, perhaps not unlike his own father had done for so many years.

153

Yet his work with alcoholics led him to open AA meetings to learn more about the disease. For thirteen years, Mac attended AA meetings while still drinking. While the truth of his disease eventually set in, he still wasn't sure he "qualified" for the program. *The Promises* assure us that God will begin to do for us what we can't do for ourselves, and so Mac was led to a treatment facility to work and study. It was there his new life began, for real.

He's now nearing the twenty-year mark since the date he turned his will and his life over to the care of God, as he had grown to understand Him. He has not looked back and has been sober ever since. The road has not always been smooth, however. The physical and emotional pain of his youth has resurfaced, and he has experienced post-traumatic stress disorder, depression, and thoughts of suicide, as well as debilitating migraines throughout his sobriety. A few years ago, he felt himself coming apart mentally and contemplated a heroin overdose. He had gotten married by this time, and his wife quietly said, "I wish you wouldn't." She said no more; she had joined Al-Anon, and her own Twelve Step program came to the aid of both of them.

Mac resisted the heroin and instead began to pray. He began to use the program in the way he had always instructed his clients to. A friend helped him see that taking the Eleventh Step and becoming willing to forgive his parents was what could and would save him. And he finally allowed others to truly care for him in a way he had never felt cared for nor had cared for himself. His AA friends came to his rescue when he asked for help, as people in the program always do when one of us is really in need. It has been a process, but Mac has been able to forgive his parents for their abuse, and as a result, he has attained peace of mind.

Mac's story shows us that no matter how dire our circumstances, no matter how impossible the odds seem to be, the grace of God can pull us back from the brink of disaster. When you have lost all hope for yourself, allowing the hope of others to carry you will serve you well. Mac knows this to be true, as does every person I interviewed for this book. My own story is also a testament of this same offering of hope. We must never doubt hope's power to save the still-suffering person, whoever he or she is.

November Suggestions for Cultivating Hope

1. We observe so much that is unloving. Practicing the assignment of responding with love and forgiveness regardless of the situation isn't easy. Count the times you did so anyway for the next week. How did this change you?

2. It isn't necessary to always be in agreement with the people around us; we can have a difference of opinion without creating discord. Observe the times you allow for the differences without creating an unnecessary argument.

3. Accepting others as they are is the surest way to peace. Practicing acceptance is a decision. Observe your willingness to do so for a week and write how this practice changed you.

4. Being willing to forgive a friend for a transgression is the balm that soothes and heals your heart. Have you had an opportunity to experience this recently? If so, describe your experience in your notebook or journal and tell someone else about it, too.

Any Unloving Action Is an Appeal for Healing and Help.

Unloving actions abound—in our homes, in the workplace, in our neighborhoods, everywhere there are people. Just think for a moment about how many of the stories on last night's local news or in this morning's paper recounted acts of violence: stories about bombs exploding in another part of the world, gang wars in American cities, and domestic violence, possibly on your own block. You or someone you know may have been a victim of violence.

It's natural to feel overwhelmed, even hopeless, by the thoughtless acts of violence we encounter in the world every day. Add to that the violence portrayed in channel after channel of television programs and at the movies playing at your local cinema, and we are bombarded—our children are bombarded—with violence. I'm sure that most of us have wondered what its effects are on us and if there's anything we can do about it. Fortunately, there is.

If we accept that unloving acts, regardless of their form, *156* are most often marks of an individual's fear and insecurity, we are given a framework for understanding them. Understanding such acts doesn't mean they become acceptable. Yet, when we become willing to see the perpetrator as fearful—perhaps due to his own childhood abuse or as the result of growing up in a cycle of violence—the resulting violence against others might become understandable, even forgivable in time. Society needs to have sanctions and means of restitution when a crime is involved, but even in these cases, an act of forgiveness, which requires only a tiny willingness, can free both the perpetrator and the victim and bring them relief and healing.

My many years of spiritual exploration brought me to a path that introduced me to an idea that comforts me daily. It's this: *every loving thought is true; everything else is an appeal for healing and/or help.* While this idea may be controversial to some people and challenge some of our traditional beliefs, it can offer a fresh perspective on the many violent images that crowd our minds. It's not easy to shift our perception from seeing as we have always seen to accommodate such a radical view. But with practice, I've found that we can apply this principle more easily than you may think, especially when we actually experience the freedom and hope that comes with opening our minds and hearts to another person with forgiveness. Being open to another way of seeing and interpreting behavior that had caused us to reject and condemn people in the past promises us that we can feel an inner peace, even while the world around us remains in chaos. We may not be able to change the chaos, but we can see through it to the hope that lies in the calls for help and healing that it masks.

157

*Seeking to see unloving actions as appeals for
healing and help softens the heart. And when our hearts
are soft, we will affect those around us in a hopeful,
peaceful way. What a week this can be if we allow
for this change in our minds and hearts.*

Forgiveness Is the Key to Real Peace of Mind.

I heard a man speak at a conference a number of years
ago, and I was amazed by what he shared. Some years prior to
this conference, two people broke into his home one evening,
thinking they would find drugs because he was a physician
with a home office. The intruders had assumed that no one
would be home, but the doctor's wife happened upon them.
Although they had not planned to hurt anyone, she surprised
them, and they responded by taking her life very violently.

His voice was very soft when he shared the story, and
he spoke with no rancor. At first I wondered if he was simply
still in shock, even though this had happened a dozen years
earlier, but it soon became apparent that the shock was gone.
And so was the anger. The killers were found and tried for
murder. He was present every day in the courtroom, he said,
and initially felt the killers deserved to die. Yet when they
were sentenced to life in prison, this brought him no peace.
He came to see that his anguish, his anger and resentment,
were killing him just as surely as the two killers had ended
158 his wife's life. He began to pray with a fervency that he'd
never felt before. At first, he prayed to be relieved of his rage.

Eventually, he began to pray for the willingness to forgive his wife's murderers.

By the time he shared this story at the conference, his life had been transformed. He not only lived in a state of forgiveness, but he had developed a relationship with one of the killers. Initially, he simply wanted to know her, he said, to understand how she could do what she did. Upon meeting her, he could see that she was as mystified by her actions as he was when he first discovered his wife's body. Her anguish was as great as his. Her horror at her actions matched his. She was just eighteen at the time of the murder, high on drugs, and homeless.

What happened next was the miracle of this whole story. He began to visit her in prison. She had no family that she knew of, and he became her connection to the outside world. Soon thereafter, he went to her aid and tried to get her released from prison or at least a new trial. He has not succeeded. She remains in prison, but every opportunity she has to go before the parole board, he accompanies her. She is transformed by his forgiveness. Just as important, he is transformed. The decision to forgive someone for whatever they may have done is the real key to peace of mind. This man had found peace of mind through forgiveness and had brought it to the person he forgave as well.

The message I took from this story was that nothing has to be unforgivable. It may take time to get where our speaker got. What he experienced was indeed tragic, but the benefit of reaching that depth of forgiveness, not only to him but to the young woman and everyone touched by their story, is beyond measure. The forgiveness any one of us carries in our hearts touches more people than we'll ever know. Forgiveness softens us and removes barriers between us and other people. To accept the idea that even the most unimaginable action can be forgiven releases an aura of hope around our hearts. And when that happens, all of humankind breathes more peacefully.

> *There is no way to overestimate the power of forgiveness.*
> *There would be a seismic shift in the world's spiritual*
> *well-being if forgiveness was on everyone's mind.*

Being Gentle Doesn't Require Agreement.

To be gentle is a choice, and not even a particularly difficult one. Being gentle is easier, in fact, than being harsh or controlling or angry. It takes less energy to be gentle and accepting, and it makes us feel so much better about who we are in the moment. It's probably true that most people feel uncomfortable when they are argumentative and adamant about getting their way. Getting the best of someone else in a disagreement generally provides only short-term gratification, if any. And it frequently calls for an apology eventually. Allowing for differences is a far more peaceful way to live. It sets such a good and hopeful example for others as well. Making gentleness our first response, especially with people we don't agree with, is a great habit to cultivate.

This isn't a principle I lived by for a good part of my life. I believed in reaching agreement all right, as long as it was *you who agreed with me!* I never knew when to let go, when to let

you be you. I based my self-esteem on whether others agre
with me or not, and needless to say, my life was generally filled
with turmoil. I lived with creeping and continuous self-doubt.
What a blessing I don't have to live that way anymore. When
we decide to be gentle responders to all the people who wander into our space, life will become so much easier. The sim-
plicity with which we can live when we make the decision to
be gentle instead of confrontational is astounding, and our
actions will affect many others, too. The irony is that it takes
so little to do so much for the well-being of so many.

It sets such a clear example for other people in our lives—
our children, our family members, our co-workers, our neighbors, and our friends near and far—when we demonstrate
gently letting go. Showing others how this is done is like
giving the gift of hope for a life free from tension. We don't
need to go around offering verbal directions on how to do
this. Showing by example is far more effective; in fact, brow-
beating people seldom changes their beliefs and behavior. But
most people do take notice of someone who seems to always
be hopeful, joyful, and gentle.

There is far too little softness in this world. Many have
been raised to believe that it is the aggressor who succeeds.
It's a definite shift in perception to choose the quieter path
among our traveling companions. If you believe as I do, that
we are always in the position to serve as teachers to one another, you might consider taking on the challenge to respond
to all situations and people, regardless of their tenor, in a kind
and gentle way. Might we dare to see how this approach could
influence the outcome of our every interaction? We can do so

much with so little effort to make this a better, more peaceful, and more hope-filled world, but we have to want to be part of the change.

> *"Signing on" to do our part is a worthwhile undertaking that ensures that tomorrow offers a better opportunity to ourselves and others. It's not difficult to do; on the contrary, it's very easy. Just practice being quieter and more gentle and offer everyone you see an example of hope that life can be free from tension.*

Acceptance Is Primary to Discovering Peace.

Discovering that our lives can be peaceful through one small (though not always simple!) act is a gift that blesses us many times a day. It's a quiet act that seldom draws attention to itself, but nonetheless it can change everything about a situation as well as our own internal sense of well-being. It's the ultimate kindness we can bestow on another human being as well as ourselves. It's called *acceptance.* Accepting the other people who travel with us, rather than trying to change them; accepting their opinions as fitting for them rather than insisting they trade them for ours; accepting that their presence signifies that we must be ready to learn something from them, or that perhaps it's time for us to give up our own treasured opinion about something—these are some of the many doorways to peace.

162

Often, acceptance includes forgiveness for an attack, whether harsh or mild—in some cases, only imagined. In any instance, not forgiving what has occurred and the person we perceive as our attacker means we will be held hostage to the situation and unable to feel peace. Nor will we experience hope. Forgiveness is a two-way street. It's not just for the person who wronged us; it's for us as well. We cannot freely accomplish anything or feel genuine hope for the present or the future if we are hanging on to something that occurred in our past. And all acts that need forgiveness are part of a past that we have chosen to hold on to in the present.

This moment that lays claim to our attention is both holy and hope-filled. There are no concerns *here*. God's presence, *here,* allows us to give up our worry over past or future events. In this moment, all is good. It is that rare exception where instant gratification is healthy for us; when, with God's help, we can revel in this very moment and let the other moments take care of themselves. Regardless of how we interpreted past events, they were meant for our growth. The same will hold true in the future. Believing this is the most hopeful decision we can make today will make all other decisions not only palatable, but understandable.

Hindsight is a wonderful teacher—this is where the past can actually serve a good purpose. Take a moment or two and remember a situation that was certain to be your undoing. Perhaps it did cause a setback, in fact. But here you are. And today you are on another leg of your journey, destined to meet the very people who are waiting for you. That's often the best sign of hope we have. God has never forsaken us. Even in our darkest times He sent "angels" to watch over us. Acceptance that God always works for our ultimate benefit—even when

163

His ways appear mysterious—frees us from the fear that this time, He won't be available. On the contrary, *if we are here, so is God.*

> *I am so grateful to have wandered into the rooms*
> *of recovery so many years ago. I was hopeless then,*
> *and now I am full of hope. The words I needed were*
> *always offered. The guidance I sought was always*
> *forthcoming, from another person, either in conversation*
> *or from a book, or more often from that still, small voice*
> *that lives in silence. God knew how to reach me even*
> *when I didn't know I was seeking Him. That's the*
> *hope we all deserve. All we have to do is be available*
> *and open to it. God takes care of the rest.*

December

LESSONS FROM GOD

*You are a child of the universe no less than
the trees and the stars; you have a right to be here . . .
The universe is unfolding as it should.*

MAX EHRMANN

⸺⚬⸺

*Seeing a Light at the End of the Tunnel
When No One Else Can.*

All of the stories in this book are close to my heart, but this one touches a chord deep within me. It's a story of resilience, love, unfaltering faith, hope, and acceptance that all things are part of the plan God has for our lives. It's Helen's story.

I met Helen more than three decades ago at a family gathering. She was my husband's widowed aunt, a second-generation Irish immigrant with a heart of gold and a gift for storytelling. Her husband, Leo, had been my father-in-law's brother; he died in the early 1950s at the age of forty-six. A painter as well as a smoker, he died of lung cancer, leaving Helen to raise their six children alone.

Much of what I share here about Helen I learned from her family and friends. Even though she and I became very good friends and card-playing companions, she was far too humble, far too quietly unaware of her successes, to tell me the details of her many accomplishments.

Helen was a nurse before she married, after which time she stayed home to raise her growing family. However, when her husband became ill, she returned to the work that had meant so much to her. Nursing helped to fill her days while the children filled her nights. Her work, along with help from Leo's large extended family, allowed Helen's family to survive. The wound in Helen's heart after Leo died remained, however.

Though she was widowed quite young and was a woman of character and natural joy, Helen never considered remarrying. She simply couldn't imagine allowing anyone to replace Leo in her life. She was kept company by fond remembrances that she loved to share, generally accompanied by hearty laughter. Every time we met to play cards, I'd look forward to new stories or even repeats of stories she had told before. Helen was a natural at storytelling—very much like Leo, I was told.

Helen never felt sorry for herself, in spite of her hardships. She never complained that life had been unfair. She believed, absolutely, that God's will was always at work in her life. She didn't doubt that it had been present in Leo's life, too. She worked hard at setting a high standard for her children to follow, and they did. All were college educated and five of the six even earned graduate degrees. Helen was proud; Leo would have been proud, too, and Helen was quite certain that he was somehow privy to their every success.

166

The first time I met Helen, I was struck by her grace and her wonderful sense of humor. She had a way of putting everyone at ease, as though you were lifelong friends. I never heard a complaint from her about anything. My own husband often called her a saint. She seemed too busy enjoying those around her to waste time complaining about conditions or people beyond her control. She set a wonderful example throughout her ninety-nine-year life, an example that's far harder to follow than Helen made it look.

When Helen was in her early nineties, her oldest daughter, Mary, died of cancer. Her death wasn't sudden, but neither was it fully expected. Throughout her illness, neither Helen nor Mary allowed the condition to get in the way of their living each minute fully, with a good measure of laughter thrown in. Mary was as cleverly irreverent as her mother was lovingly and peacefully devout, even in the toughest of times. The two women were great friends, in spite of their many differences. Helen's acceptance of everyone's opinion most likely contributed to their close relationship.

I had many great times with Mary before her death. Together, we laughed at the absurdities of life. We shared similar opinions about politics, religion, and people in the news. I always looked forward to her trips home to visit family, when she and I always found time for coffee or dinner. Her death was a huge loss to all of us, particularly to Helen. Mary, the first born, the first in Helen's family to earn a Ph.D., had made Helen so proud. But just as she had accepted the death of Leo forty years before, she knew that Mary was free now from her diseased body. She accepted her daughter's death as necessary to God's plan for her life. She shed tears, plenty of them, but she didn't feel that God was being unjust. She didn't see herself as the victim of anything or anyone. There was a plan unfolding, and she was grateful to know that. This knowledge filled her with hope. She was quite certain that her passing would be part of the same plan, when the time was right.

I was in awe of Helen's perspective on life and the inevitability of death. She believed that death took only one's body, not one's spirit, which was an expression of a greater Spirit. And it was that Spirit that she felt in communion with whenever she missed the presence of Leo and Mary. It's Helen's spirit that I now try to commune with when I am missing her. Helen died peacefully at ninety-nine, not ill, just tired. Macular degeneration had taken away her ability to read, something she had done avidly her whole life. It also took away her ability to play cards, which she missed even more than reading. As I mentioned before, she and I were bridge partners, and I miss, a lot, the times we had laughing, eating, and playing bridge. I learned so much from her at the bridge table—very little of which had to do with the game of bridge. She knew how to live life peacefully, and I wanted what she had.

One of the key things a life like Helen's demonstrates is that any adversity can be accepted as the next "right thing" on our journey. The adversities in her life were numerous. The deaths of Leo and Mary, though the toughest perhaps, were only the beginning of the long list of people she would bury before her stay here was complete. All of Helen's siblings as well as her in-laws passed on before her time had come. And yet, she put them all in perspective. She never doubted for a moment that she would see them "on the other side." She helped me to believe that, too.

When it was necessary to leave her home and move into an apartment, and later an assisted-living facility, she did so with grace and an eagerness that relieved everyone. Her final move into a nursing home was hardest on the family, because they knew the next step. Of course, Helen did, too. Yet again, with ease and grace, she allowed everyone to adjust to what she knew was inevitable. I visited her a number of times in the nursing home, and each time, her frailty was a bit more pronounced. However, her eagerness to visit, to hear about my life and what I had written most recently, and to know when I might come again gave me hope that her end wasn't as close as I knew in my heart it likely was. Every time I visited, I thought it might be for the last time.

Helen surprised us all. She was shy of one hundred by only two months when she quietly died. She generally told others she was one hundred already, in fact. I pondered that many times, wondering if she perhaps thought she had already passed that mark of achievement or if she simply wanted to make it to that glorious age. Either way, she died as gracefully and as quietly as she lived. Her lesson to all of us is that no matter what befalls you, you can accept it with the help of the presence of your Higher Power. With God's help, all things are not only possible, but can become the necessary turning points in the journey we are here to make. Her journey had many detours and multiple heartaches, but she steadfastly moved forward regardless. She never conveyed any doubt that she was being cared for and that her journey was "as ordered."

What Helen did with her life, spiritually grounded though she was, is no more and no less than what each one of us can do. As was true for Helen, we have all been prepared for whatever comes. Curve balls don't come at us that we haven't been readied for. Indeed, they may stretch us, but we are prepared for them. This simple truth is all that's necessary to live peacefully. If belief is your stumbling block right now, let the likes of Helen hold out the belief to you. Let her strength strengthen you. Her spirit, our Spirit, is willing; I promise you this.

December Suggestions for Cultivating Hope

1. Resistance to a suggestion or a person prevents the growth you deserve. Make the decision to welcome all that is moving toward you. How are you being changed? Write what you observe about yourself.

2. Among the things that have happened today or this week, both big and small, which provided the most obvious lessons for your journey? How have you been changed by them?

3. Seeing yourself in others can be painful. At the end of every day for a week, write a few notes about who you saw and what you learned about yourself.

4. Would you consider yourself hopeful? What do you see as evidence of the presence of hope, or its lack? Write a plan for things you can change right now that will make your life more hopeful.

Resist Nothing—a Lesson Is Always Being Offered.

This idea may seem preposterous. Many of our experiences nearly pushed us beyond our limits to survive. Every one of us can revisit our past and, with little trouble, create doubt about whether one or another experience was really necessary for our growth. But those who are far wiser than I am have convinced me that not a single experience lacked value in the formation of who I am today—not a single one. If I resist fully embracing an experience as a necessary opportunity for learning, it will revisit my thoughts until my wisdom overshadows my willfulness and I realize its importance.

This is a book about cultivating hope, and I think the idea that all experiences present lessons we specifically need—and that they will remain ours forever as the substance of who we are becoming—is the most hopeful message it offers. What this means, quite simply, is that we need not run from anything; nothing needs to alarm us or make us cower. Being overwhelmed is a choice we can make, but it's an unnecessary one. What is being offered to us comes with a Guide and therefore a "guidebook." Making the decision to incorporate, with trust, the experiences that have presented themselves is how we reveal our willingness to follow the *will* of the One who knows more than we know.

Men and women generally come into the rooms of AA and Al-Anon, as well as other Twelve Step programs, in a state of hopelessness. Had their lives been successful in every regard, they would not have sought the "miracle" that's available in these rooms. When they arrive, they learn that the real miracle is contained in the small word *hope*. Without it, nothing changes. With it, nothing stays the same. And as long as they stay the course, they will develop it as we have done before them.

Hope is the breath of fresh air that allows for a new perspective. Hope is the awareness that never are we alone. It's the reminder that believing there is good in all situations and people makes it possible to perceive it. Without hope, we will not move forward, fulfilling the role we have been created to play.

As I share in my own story, I was offered a new perspective about thirty minutes before I attempted to take my own life late in my first year of recovery. The terror I had lived with for so long prior to getting into recovery had returned, and I felt utterly hopeless. As I prepared to turn on the gas on the oven, there was a knock at the door, and the woman walked into my kitchen who was to change my life by offering me a new idea and, more important, hope. I will never forget how profoundly different I felt as the result of having hope once again—a substantive, lasting hope that was to sustain me until today. The beauty of what happened to me is that I have been able to share this story with others on many occasions, and that's how hope is multiplied.

> *We don't all feel hope all the time, but when any one of*
> *us shares an experience that brought hope into our lives,*
> *it allows others to know there's a reason to claim it*
> *for themselves. Let today be that day for you.*

We Are Both Students and Teachers.

While it's true that all of us are teachers as well as students, the ultimate teacher, of course, is God. Our real work in this life is to listen to God's message, be good stewards of it, share what we have learned with others when appropriate, and lend a helping hand to other people on our path who haven't heard the message as clearly as we have. Our work is pretty well defined and not very complicated: it is to spread hope where it is in short supply.

I remember struggling to know what God's will was for me when I was introduced to the Twelve Steps of Alcoholics Anonymous and then Al-Anon nearly thirty-five years ago. A friend, someone I knew outside of the fellowship who recognized my turmoil, asked, "Do you believe that God is love?" I said of course. Then he asked, "Can you accept that will and thought are the same?" This, too, made sense to me. His next comment offered me the much-needed solace I craved, and his words eased my discontent. "God's *will* is *loving thought*. Nothing more," he said. I breathed a sigh of hope and felt like I could proceed with my life.

I have carried my friend's words and this idea tucked away in my heart ever since. *One loving thought at a time is all we have to nurture and pass on to others.* I knew he was right and this was so manageable. The lesson he shared came directly from God, I am certain of this, and it has been passed on by me thousands of times, too. I was my friend's student. God had been his teacher and was my teacher, too, through him. And then the circle widened. That's how it is with hope. It goes from one to another and then another.

When we receive a message that offers gentle guidance and much-needed hope in a troubling time, God is the primary teacher. The person sharing the thought is a steward, an assignment and role we all get to play every day. Knowing that our work is never done and that our job is always to serve others in the most loving way makes life pretty simple and our purpose quite obvious. How well planned our lives actually are.

Not all of God's lessons are immediately clearly discernible or easy to accept. Occasionally, a "lesson" may even remove us from a situation we thought was right for us, such as a relationship or a job, and we feel threatened. But coming to believe that God is always directing the orchestra and we are simply playing the instrument we've been given gives us peace. Keeping our thoughts loving and trusting serves God, our fellow travelers, and ourselves, too. God never removes from us what is in our best interests. We are not always the best judge of what's right for us. But we are able to discern the difference between a loving thought and one that's fearful or judgmental. God is available to show us the difference if we should ever forget.

God's primary lesson is to trust and offer the hand
of love to others. When we do this, we can be assured
that we will be directed to the outcome that is the
most beneficial for everyone sharing our journey.
May you find this so in your life today.

We See Ourselves in Everyone,
and Not Always Happily So.

Have you ever wondered why you meet so many difficult people on your journey? We encounter these men and women everywhere we go—in our neighborhoods, at work, at social gatherings, perhaps at the gym, at the grocery or hardware store, and in our own living rooms and kitchens! We know the types who trouble us: opinionated, pushy, rudely dismissive, controlling, whiny. It doesn't matter what the behavior is; it's that we allow their behavior to control our feelings and even undermine our self-esteem. It's said that we give others rent-free space in our minds when we let their behavior define who we are in the moment—and worse, when their actions actually determine our reactions.

What if I said that every one of these cranky individuals, along with all of the pleasant people we meet, are present for two reasons? First, they show us the many sides of ourselves. We always see in others qualities we share, sometimes buried deep beneath our surface, sometimes evident to anyone. This idea isn't easily embraced, but teachers far wiser than I have convinced me it's true, and coming to accept this truth has made me more willing to change in ways I had never before considered. And the second reason these people are present is that *everyone* present is our next obvious opportunity for offering an expression of love. That thought eases my mind and touches my heart. Though not always easy, making the expression of love my reason for being with whoever is present has made my life far less stressful. This practice has also given me hope

175

that within the tiny spaces of every experience, something good can happen for each person. Whoever stands before us is "on assignment," and we have an assignment, too. Rather than judging, we will be extending hope by reaching out with love.

Being aware that the qualities we react to in others are also in us provides a nice way for making potentially troubling encounters smoother. Monitoring our own defects by what we judge to be defects in others is also a readily accessible way to do a personal inventory. And this applies to assets, too! We would not see those assets, the kindnesses of others, if we didn't also share those qualities. This insight is something to savor.

While it's true that the good and the bad that we see in others mirror who we are, let's remember that whatever we observe is for our own learning and self-awareness and is not meant to either shame us *or* make us prideful. Every quality we see allows us the opportunity to embrace it and strengthen it, or willingly release it so that our next action is one we can feel good about. The give-and-take of our interactions every waking moment is fraught with opportunity. We are on a mission; so are our compatriots. Isn't it a wonderful mystery how we have gathered to learn from one another, to stretch one another, to honor one another, and to love one another?

There is no greater gift we can pass on to others
than to hold hope in our hearts for the peaceful life
of each one of us. We can do this best when we have
embraced whatever our individual struggles may be.
There is no time like the present to begin.

Hope Opens the Door to the Solution We Seek.

We cannot find solutions for our problems if we live in the chaos; we need to venture through the door marked "hope." Solutions await us there. It seems like such a simple decision, but making that decision eludes us so easily. Living in the problem becomes a habit for many. Even when others tell us *there is another way,* many of us remain stuck, often for years. This was certainly true of me.

But then for some of us, a shift finally occurs, and we decide to stop living in the space of hopelessness. At that moment, everything changes, and nothing will ever look the same again. We become guides for others, teaching them as others have taught us. Were it not for those wiser than us, little would ever change in our lives. A good friend suggested I go to Al-Anon many decades ago. That was my new beginning. But old habits die hard; new perceptions seem so foreign. *"What do you mean I can't change anyone else?"*

In actuality, we don't ever have to change. We get to make that decision. Most of us know people who have stayed in the same hopeless situation for years, oftentimes complaining bitterly and always blaming someone else for their miserable circumstances. But these people have the same opportunity available to all of us: to switch gears and learn the lesson that comes with every experience. We are not held hostage to a particular mind-set except by choice.

This is one of the key principles I've woven throughout this book: every experience we have is the next right opportunity for a valuable lesson. And it is a lesson that keeps on giving as the people around us benefit when we change our thoughts and behavior. What comfort that our lives have been so perfectly planned and that we are the necessary parts in this Greater Whole that moves each of us closer to the moment of true enlightenment. What we don't understand now, we will fully absorb when the time is right. Until then, our work includes building trust so that we may become willing demonstrations of the better, more peaceful way to perceive the world around us. And little by little, we will change, and as we change, we will be able to see those changes happening in others, too.

The problems that come knocking on our door are there for a reason, and none will be too big to handle if we can let others guide us who can see the solution we think we're lacking. There will always be others who have already walked through similar difficult circumstances and can show us how to gain the strength to face any problem by placing our trust in our Higher Power and those around us who are His emissaries.

Lessons big and small will come calling as long as we live. And we will be given the opportunity to choose again and again to be both grateful students and willing teachers, a beacon of hope for others that Love is the solution to every problem.

Hope sustains us so that we may choose love over fear.
As you cultivate hope in your life, share it with others.
There is no greater work today.

Concluding Thoughts

It has been said—and proven time and again—that wherever we are is where we can make a difference in the life of someone else. I have come to believe that our real purpose *here* is to make that difference. It doesn't have to be a big difference. Even a smile can change the outlook for someone we see on the street, or offering a comforting touch of the hand or arm to a friend who seems troubled.

Carl Jung used the term *synchronicity* to describe the "meaningful coincidences" that bring people together who are meant to share a moment in space and time. We need not worry about the orchestration—that part has already been planned. And the outcome of the meeting is left in the hands of the Greater Power who saw reason for the meeting. Our part is to be grateful for the "invitation" and then the willingness to do as bidden.

Whether our circumstances allow us to directly touch hundreds of people or only one, we each have a part to play in how this story gets told. It's my hope that this small book has shown you how easily any one of us can influence, in a positive way, the journey of a fellow traveler. And when the journey of any one of us changes for the good, it will be felt by everyone, everywhere, in time. This is a truth we can trust.

Additional Reflections for Months with an Extra Week

Hopefulness Is Contagious.

Support groups offer hope to millions of people worldwide. Perhaps that's their most important contribution to peaceful living. People come to these groups because they have run out of ideas for solving their crises on their own. While most self-help groups refrain from solving the particular crisis, they do demonstrate, by the personal experiences of their members, that there is no problem too big to be handled. And they do assure us that everyone present has felt at some time like you, the newcomer, feel now. There is such relief in that awareness. Being alone in our pain is not our only option. We can share our pain, and it will be halved, immediately. Conversely, when people share their hope, it will be doubled, and we learn that our lives can change.

Sensing hope in others is like a breath of fresh air when we are caught in the trappings of a problem. We are lifted by the belief that situations will improve for us when those we sit among recount times when they have been down, but would not be counted out. It offers a fascinating commentary on the human condition. The power of something as elusive as hope, as indescribable as it often is, can transform how we feel about a situation. Hope is, perhaps, the forerunner of any life-changing decision. The belief that something better is available—and that we deserve that "something better"—starts the ball rolling in a new direction. Transformation of ourselves, along with the situation troubling us, is right around the corner when we dare to hope. And when we can muster up the willingness to hope, we can allow others to carry hope for us.

Moods are contagious. A raucous gathering can easily breed some form of acting out in the quietest person present. Or someone's overwhelming sadness can easily elicit a similar response in a person sharing the experience. Sociologists have pointed to how easily, and how frequently, a full-scale riot has developed from the violent acts of a few. The same can be said for the power of hope. We are moved by its presence in the people around us, and we move others by our expression of it on their behalf. We do not have to feel hope in the moment ourselves for hope to change the moment for us. The quiet power of hope can penetrate our lives through those who journey with us through our troubling experiences.

No difficult situation can hold us down indefinitely if we allow even a hint of hope to get our attention. A job loss can be managed if we believe that a better opportunity awaits us. A failed marriage, though devastating, can become the door opener for finding a more enduring love. Even though we might feel overcome with hopelessness in the midst of these experiences, we can quiet our own turmoil by allowing others to hold hope in their hearts for us until we can cultivate it ourselves.

Anyone's willingness to hope benefits everyone alive.
Like the never-ending ripple in a lake caused by one tiny
tossed pebble, hope, too, can spread into each of our
hearts. The critical mass will be reached when enough
of us offer a hopeful heart, a hopeful hand, and
a hopeful prayer for someone in need.

Every Person Is a Messenger.
Seek the Hope in the Message.

This principle leaves no one out of the equation. Every friend, acquaintance, and stranger is a messenger who has *come calling* for a reason. Although this idea has been discussed already, it's worth considering again because of its enormous impact on our individual and collective lives. Everyone who reaches out to us has a message worthy of our attention. In fact, it's a message we have been waiting for! We may not realize this at the moment the words are shared, but we will come to understand their full importance before long. What we learn from each messenger is what we are then prepared to share, in some way, with those who look to us. This is a glorious awareness when fully absorbed. The cycle of hope is unending. We give away that which we have received.

The idea that an element of hope lies within every message we receive may seem to be a stretch if the words we hear initiate fear or dread in us. Perhaps the messenger is our boss, for instance, and the message is that we are being laid off. When we resist the message, particularly one that's dire, we generally

183

do so because we have forgotten that God is part of every equation. No message, and no messenger, comes to us alone or unintentionally. The simple truth is we need not be afraid. We can trust that the words shared are meant to inform us about something significant, to prepare us for what is coming next. We are never being given a message that's meaningless. The hope contained within the message is ours to perceive.

Believing this takes faith. That all messages can, in the final analysis, be considered hopeful requires more than simple acceptance. We may need to become willing to disregard what our fearful ego (that noisy voice in our minds) is telling us about the messenger. Some messages may seem unloving and discounting of our plans, but then how often do we know for sure where we are *supposed* to be going next? Most of us didn't expect to be where we are now, and maybe, just maybe, the message before us is exactly what we need to hear to make the next right decision in our lives. This has certainly been true for me. When my first husband left, I hated his parting words, but they did usher in a whole new life for me, one that I am so grateful for. I had not planned on ending up *here,* but I am nonetheless delighted.

There is hope to be gleaned from every experience and every messenger. At times, we have to be patient, trust in the process, and know that the God of our understanding will not lead us astray. We have always ended up where we needed to be, eventually. And this will always be the case. Listen for your guide to tell you what you need to know right now. He or she will be heading your way, *is* heading your way, in fact, right now. Be faithful—be full of faith.

184

What an exciting journey we are on.
We are being given the very "directions" we need
to live fully, fruitfully, and with hope in our hearts.
We will not meet anyone accidentally. Everyone has
come as bidden to the encounter with us. Let's relish
the truth of this and go forth today joyfully.

We Know Forgiveness When We Listen to the Quieter Voice.

We must be willing to forgive others if we want peace in our lives. In some instances, it seems impossible initially. Being a victim of sexual, physical, or emotional harm and abuse can haunt a person for decades. It doesn't seem reasonable or justified to forgive the perpetrator, particularly if our lives were jeopardized. But dwelling on these "unforgivable" acts eventually holds us hostage. We need to ask ourselves if that's how we want to live. We risk giving up all hope for a contented life if we stay in the painful baggage of the past.

Life happens, and we all experience a host of seemingly unnecessary and unfair insults and attacks from people we know and trust and from strangers. These can range from the unspeakable to mere affronts and simple misunderstandings. I am not suggesting we quickly stamp our approval on any of them; however, letting whatever happened fester in our minds prohibits the growth we were born to experience. Nor will it allow us to fulfill our calling to be role models of God's peace and forgiveness in the lives of others who cross our path.

185

They have "appeared" because of their need for connection, for whatever guidance our own experiences have trained us to give. If we are trapped in our past—and any unforgiveness is related to the past—we will not have the foresight or the willingness to offer the hope that another person deserves the moment they arrive on our path.

Forgiveness is a decision. It's not one that is made easily. Prayer and meditation are generally required before we reach that space in our minds when we can let go of our hurt—but we *can* let it go. Most of us have observed others who have let go of horrible wrongs done to them in their past. I have been privy to the story of a woman who forgave the drunk driver who killed her child. She wrote to him throughout his prison term, an act that she feels now saved her own life. I am not suggesting it's easy, but it can be done. Can we do it? That's the question we have to ask ourselves.

Forgiveness is what opens the door to the good life we hope for and that is our inheritance from God. Victimhood serves no one. It doesn't resolve past hurts and harms; rather, it makes the past loom larger. And it doesn't punish anyone but ourselves. We will know no peace and fulfill few, if any, of our dreams, if we hang on to old hurts. As unfortunate and painful as these hurts may be, they all have the capacity to teach us something, too. For certain, we don't have to be defined by what happened. Although it's usually true that people who are hurt tend to hurt others, the perpetrators of harms in our past aren't defined solely by what they did, either. There's more to each one of us than our pasts, even if that past seems to instill in us the propensity to hurt other travelers on the

186

path. That's what we need to remember about ourselves and, finally, to forgive in others when the circumstance calls for it.

Hope, the gift we receive from our attempts at forgiveness, will change every tomorrow of our lives.

Forgiveness Is the Most Treasured Gift We Can Offer Another.

We've all heard it said that "cleanliness is next to godliness"; I think it's more accurate to say that "forgiveness is next to godliness." What an appealing idea. Holding on to resentments against anyone—whether friends, foes, or perfect strangers—prevents us from feeling hopeful about the circumstances currently calling for our attention. We really can't hold on to more than one idea at a time, and if the one we are nurturing isn't based in love, then we are adding not only to our own immediate chaos but also to the chaos of the world.

Many philosophers and spiritual teachers have assured us since ancient times that our lives are interconnected. Now, starting with the discoveries of quantum mechanics, modern science is also teaching this to us. Fundamentally, we do not exist as distinctly separate entities, nor are we separate from the very activities we are involved in or are observing. Heisenberg's Principle of Uncertainty laid the scientific foundation for this idea in 1927. Restated as a spiritual law, we can say that we are affecting and being affected all the time by the actions, the thoughts, even the prayers of others.

That's the good *and* the bad of our existence, actually. And yet, for every negative action someone is taking, for every selfish, mean-spirited thought spewed out, we can shift the world back into balance by exerting the same effort for good. Of course, this means we all have a very important role to play, one that matters not just to the safety and well-being of our loved ones, but to the comfort of those we will never physically encounter. We are all needed. We all have a gift to offer the world. We are not superfluous to the moment at hand.

We all want to matter to one another, and an act of forgiveness can fulfill this desire every day. Hanging on to even the tiniest of resentments—and we all have them—diminishes our hope for forgiveness for ourselves. We simply can't be hopeful and resentful in the same moment. We must choose. Knowing that we have the capacity to add to the blessings affecting all of God's creatures makes the right choice evident.

That hope is absent in the lives of so many, including those we know personally, is our direct invitation to make a difference here and now. People who need our help do not appear in our lives by accident. We can offer help in a way that doesn't cost money or require much time. We can practice the art of holding out hope for others when they can't seem to muster it for themselves. At times, this may take the form of prayer. When we see someone struggling in any way, we can say a quiet prayer that their mind and their life can be changed. We can say a prayer that they might become willing to allow a shift in their perception for the possibilities that could unfold in their life.

Hope is available as a gift to be given and received, and as a prayer to be offered. When we contemplate all that we have to be grateful for, it increases our capacity to be hopeful for the days ahead. We can be grateful in the knowledge that no matter who we are or what we've done, the same forgiving God who has brought you and me this far won't ever abandon us. That's hope realized. Do you have enough to share?

About the Author

KAREN CASEY, PH.D., is a noted author, speaker, and workshop presenter. Her workshops have been offered throughout the United States, Canada, Ireland, Germany, and Mexico. She penned her first book, *Each Day a New Beginning: Daily Meditations for Women,* in 1982. Since then, she has published an additional twenty-one books. She served on the board of trustees for the Hazelden Foundation, was vice president and publisher for Hazelden, and currently serves as the moderator for Hazelden's Women Healing series of conferences. She has been in the rooms of recovery for thirty-five years. Karen and her husband, Joe, divide their time between Minnesota and Florida. To read more about Karen and her books, go to www .womens-spirituality.com.

Hazelden, a national nonprofit organization founded in 1949, helps people reclaim their lives from the disease of addiction. Built on decades of knowledge and experience, Hazelden offers a comprehensive approach to addiction that addresses the full range of patient, family, and professional needs, including treatment and continuing care for youth and adults, research, higher learning, public education and advocacy, and publishing.

A life of recovery is lived "one day at a time." Hazelden publications, both educational and inspirational, support and strengthen lifelong recovery. In 1954, Hazelden published *Twenty-Four Hours a Day,* the first daily meditation book for recovering alcoholics, and Hazelden continues to publish works to inspire and guide individuals in treatment and recovery, and their loved ones. Professionals who work to prevent and treat addiction also turn to Hazelden for evidence-based curricula, informational materials, and videos for use in schools, treatment programs, and correctional programs.

Through published works, Hazelden extends the reach of hope, encouragement, help, and support to individuals, families, and communities affected by addiction and related issues.

For questions about Hazelden publications,
please call **800-328-9000** or visit us online at
hazelden.org/bookstore.